WITHDRAWN

The Aquinas Lecture, 1961

METAPHYSICS
AND
HISTORICITY

Under the Auspices of the Aristotelian Society
of Marquette University

by

EMIL L. FACKENHEIM, Ph.D.

MARQUETTE UNIVERSITY PRESS
MILWAUKEE
1961

Library of Congress Catalogue Number: 61-10054

Third Printing, 1975

ISBN 0-87462-126-7

To Rose

Prefatory

The Aristotelian Society of Marquette University each year invites a scholar to deliver a lecture in honor of St. Thomas Aquinas. Customarily delivered on a Sunday close to March 7, the feast day of the society's patron saint, the lectures are called the Aquinas lectures.

In 1961 the Aquinas lecture "Metaphysics and Historicity" was delivered on March 5 in the Peter A. Brooks Memorial Union of Marquette University by Dr. Emil L. Fackenheim, associate professor of the Department of Philosophy, University of Toronto.

Dr. Fackenheim was born in Halle, Germany in 1916 and studied at the Universities of Halle, Germany; Aberdeen, Scotland; and Toronto, Canada. He was ordained a Rabbi at Berlin in 1939 and received his Ph.D. degree from the University of Toronto in 1945.

A member of the Philosophy department at the University of Toronto since 1948, Dr. Fackenheim, a Guggenheim Fellow in 1957-58, has written over sixty articles and reviews. In 1954 he received the President's Medal of the University of Western Ontario for the best scholarly article published in Canada during that year. The article was "Kant and Radical Evil," *University of Toronto Quarterly*, XXIII, pp. 339-53.

Among his other writing are the following:

"The Conception of Substance in the Philosophy of the *Ikhwan as-Safa* (Brethren of Purity)," *Mediaeval Studies*, V (1943), pp. 115-22.

" 'A Treatise on Love,' by Ibn Sina, translated from the Arabic, with Introduction and Notes," *Mediaeval Studies*, VII (1945), pp. 208-28.

"The Possibility of the Universe in al-Farabi, Ibn Sina and Maimonides," *Proceedings of the American Academy for Jewish Research*, XVI (1947), pp. 39-70.

"Mediaeval Jewish Philosophy," in V. Ferm, *A History of Philosophical Systems* (New York: The Philosophical Library, 1950) pp. 171-84.

"Schelling's Philosophy of Religion," *University of Toronto Quarterly,* XXII (1952), pp. 1-17.

"Schelling's Philosophy of the Literary Arts," *The Philosophical Quarterly,* IV (1954), pp. 310-26.

"Schelling's Conception of Positive Philosophy," *The Review of Metaphysics,* VII (1954), pp. 563-82.

"Kant's Concept of History," *Kant-Studien,* XLVIII (1957), pp. 381-98.

"Jewish Existence and the Living God," in A. Rose, *A People and Its Faith* (Toronto: University of Toronto Press, 1959), pp. 105-18.

To the list of his writings the Aristotelian Society has the pleasure of adding *Metaphysics and Historicity.*

Acknowledgements

There are many reasons why I am deeply grateful for the invitation to deliver this lecture: the opportunity to pay tribute to the great metaphysician in whose honor it is given, the admission to a company of distinguished lecturers, and the gracious hospitality of Marquette University. But I appreciate above all the rare opportunity to address an audience which will not be baffled or dismayed by the straightforward use of metaphysical language. Early in the nineteenth century, Hegel made an apt remark about the then fashionable view that in order for metaphysics to be legitimate, prior epistemological justification is needed. He compared it to the desire of the legendary student who wished to learn how to swim before going into the water. Hegel's comparison might be applied to the currently fashionable view that in order for metaphysical language to be meaningful, there is need for prior semantic or linguistic justification. I am happy to be addressing an audience which knows that metaphysical language can be understood, justified and criticized only in the actual process of metaphysical discourse.

An earlier version of a small portion of this lecture was delivered, under the title "On Nature and History," at the ninth annual meeting of the Metaphysical Society of America, on March 29, 1958, at Providence, R.I.

I wish to thank the Oxford University Press, for permission to quote a lengthy passage from Erich Frank, *Philosophical Understanding and Religious Truth* (New York: 1945); and the Princeton University Press, for permission to quote an even lengthier passage from Walter Lowrie's translation of S. Kierkegaard's *Either/Or* (Princeton: 1944).

Metaphysics and Historicity

History is a predicament for man who must live in it. In order to act in history he must seek to rise above it. He needs perspectives in terms of which to understand his situation, and timeless truths and values in terms of which to act in it. Yet the perspectives which he finds often merely reflect his age; and what he accepts as timelessly true and valid is apt to be merely the opinion which is in fashion. Thus while man must always try to rise above his historical situation he succeeds at best only precariously.

This predicament, always part of the human condition, is felt by contemporary Western man more keenly than by man in any previous age. This is in part because of the breath-taking swiftness of contemporary events. Never have men had so much cause to seek a transcending wisdom in terms of which to understand and influence the course of events, and yet to fear that such a wisdom is beyond their reach. For never has yesterday's wisdom become stale so quickly, and hence has present counsel been regarded with so much doubt.

This effect of contemporary events is reinforced by an intellectual development which, in the West, began in the nineteenth century. For a century and a half, Western man has developed an ever increasing historical self-consciousness. And this has not been without grave spiritual effects. In earlier ages, most men could simply accept religious beliefs or moral principles, as unquestionably true. In this historically self-conscious age, few men can ever forget that what seems unquestionably true to one age or civilization differs from what seems unquestionably true to others. And from historical self-consciousness there is but one step—albeit a long and fateful one

—to a wholesale historical scepticism: to the despairing view that history discloses a variety of conflicting *Weltanschauungen,* with no criterion for choice between them anywhere in sight. But when events move as they do today this step is easily taken.[1]

1.　For the development of modern Western historical consciousness, cf. especially F. Meinecke, *Die Entstehung des Historismus* (Munich: Oldenbourg, 1936).

　　Gerhard Krueger describes the predicament of history as follows: "We are able to inquire into history only while being part of it. We seek permanent truths about history; yet we ourselves, our whole thinking included, are nothing permanent. This is the predicament of history, radically stated: that we are so changeable and yet are in such need of the permanent." *Grundfragen der Philosophie* (Frankfurt: Vittorio Klostermann, 1958), p. 49. Krueger describes the development of Western awareness of this predicament as follows. The Greeks had not yet discovered it. Thinkers such as St. Augustine coped with it in terms of the Christian doctrine of Providence. The Enlightenment dealt with it in terms of the belief in progress. Because it was first to abandon the belief in the superiority of the present over the past, Romanticism was first to discover the predicament of history; but both Romanticism and German Idealism sought to resolve it by rising above history into timelessness. Because the belief in the possibility of such a rise is no longer acceptable in the present age, this age is "an age

Just how commonly it is in fact taken may be illustrated by a review of three typically contemporary attitudes. The first is what may be called *sceptical paralysis.* Here historical self-consciousness has led to two results: to the insight that wherever there has been a great purpose there has been a great faith; and to the loss of capacity for commitment to such a faith. Hence there is paralysis which recognizes itself as paralysis and preaches doom.[2]

Then there is what may be called *pragmatic make-believe.* Here man, caught in scepticism, seeks escape from its paralyzing consequences. Unable to believe and yet seeking a purpose, he falls to pretend-

of total historicity," one of "mutually incompatible standpoints." *Ibid.*, p. 8. This lecture will make clear that we do not wholly agree with Krueger's account; we have summarized it here because it is profoundly challenging.

2. The first great warning against the possible ill-effects of a strongly developed historical self-consciousness was given in 1874, in Nietzsche's *Use and Abuse of History.* The most famous literary document which illustrates these effects is Oswald Spengler's *The Decline of the West* (London: Allen and Unwin, 1926-28).

ing to believe, hoping that a pretended might do the work of an actual faith. But it cannot. For a pretended faith is no faith at all. Pragmatic make-believe collapses in self-contradiction.[3]

3.   Contemporary manifestations of pragmatic make-believe are so common as to leave one at a loss which to cite as an example. As apt as any is the current North American search for a purpose, when what is wanted is not a truth which commands dedication, but merely an effective tool in the struggle against neurosis, juvenile delinquency or cold war foes. Such a tool, if it is merely a tool, is foredoomed to ineffectiveness.

Commenting on pragmatic make-believe in its religious application, Erich Frank writes: "If we believe in . . . God not because He is the truth, but assume His truth only because we believe in Him, then there are as many gods and as many truths and values as there are beliefs. In that case, pluralism is the inescapable consequence, and it remains for the individual and his liking to choose his own truth and his own God. . . . This subjective concept of belief is a contradiction in itself. A belief that believes only in itself is no longer a belief. For true belief transcends itself; it is a belief in something—in a truth which is not determined by faith but which, on the contrary, determines faith." *Philosophical Understanding and Religious Truth* (London-New York-Toronto: O x f o r d University Press, 1945), pp. 42-43.

The pragmatic is by no means to be confused with the existentialist concept of religious truth.

When men truly suffer from this contradiction they may seek escape in the most ominous form of modern spiritual life: *ideological fanaticism.* Unlike pragmatic make-believe and like faith, ideology asserts itself absolutely. But unlike faith and like pragmatic make-believe, it is shot through with historical scepticism. For it knows itself to be not truth, but merely one specific product of history.

Hence unlike faith, ideology must by its very nature become fanatical. When chal-

The latter does not assert that commitment *makes* a belief true. It asserts that only in commitment can a person discover whether a belief *is* true, and hence—since commitment is "subjective" whereas the truth to which it commits itself is "objective" (if it is truth at all)—that all religious commitment is shot through with risk. Thus Abraham's predicament, as expounded in Kierkegaard's *Fear and Trembling* (Garden City, N.Y.: Doubleday, 1954), is that *if* God commands him to sacrifice Isaac, then this commandment is "objective," i.e., valid quite independently of Abraham's belief or lack of belief; but that, at the same time, Abraham has no standards other than his own "subjective" belief in terms of which to decide whether the commandment is objective and divine, or the mere product of his own imagination.

lenged by a conflicting faith, faith may
withdraw on its certainty of *being* true.
Because it knows itself to be but one product of history, ideology can achieve certainty only by *making* itself true; and this
it can do absolutely only by re-creating all
history in its own image. When challenged, therefore, ideology cannot withdraw on itself; it must seek to destroy the
challenger. That is, in order to resolve its
internal conflict between absolute assertion and historical scepticism, it must en-
gage in a total war from which it hopes to
emerge as the only ideology left on earth.[4]

4. So long as "belief which believes only in itself" (cf. note 3) still believes in *one* thing beyond itself—democratic tolerance—it will tolerate
a pluralism of beliefs. It is when the overwhelming need for certainty and absoluteness destroys
this one remaining belief that "belief which believes only in itself" turns into ideological fanaticism. On the connection between scepticism and
fanaticism, cf. Karl Jaspers, *Philosophie* (Berlin:
Springer-Verlag, 1948), p. 208. On the most
demonic form of contemporary ideological fanaticism, cf. Hermann Rauschning, *The Revolution
of Nihilism* (New York: Longmans, Green and
Company, 1939).
　　Perhaps the most arresting account of totali-

HISTORY AND METAPHYSICAL TRUTH

Such, then, are the disastrous effects of historical scepticism on the present age. One asks: is the long and fateful step from historical self-consciousness to historical scepticism an inevitable step? Or is it, on the contrary, a mis-step to be avoided at all costs—the mere result of confusion and failure of nerve?

tarianism is Hannah Arendt's *The Origins of Totalitarianism* (New York: Meridian Books, 1958). Among the countless insights offered in this brilliant work is the close and indeed inseparable connection, in totalitarianism, between nihilism, ideology, fanaticism and the perpetuity of "movement." It was an essential part of Nazism to assert "the futility of everything that is an end in itself" (*ibid.*, p. 323); for only then could the deified "movement of history" be absolute and all-embracing. Yet this "movement" was itself devoid of definable ends toward which it was directed; for only thus could the "Fuehrer's" authority have the kind of absoluteness which included the defining and arbitrary redefining of every "program" as whim dictated. It was therefore not at all out of character that men such as Hitler and Goebbels should, in the end, have expressed ghoulish satisfaction at the prospect that their downfall might carry in train the doom, not only—or even at all—of their enemies, but of the "master-race."

Asking this question, one cannot avoid turning to that most ancient of all philosophical enterprises, metaphysics. For in its long and eventful career, metaphysics has made one claim without hesitation and with the utmost consistency: that the predicament of history, however grave, is not wholly beyond human remedy; that at least when engaged in metaphysical discourse, man can rise above history to a grasp of timeless truth. Such a metaphysician as St. Thomas Aquinas may have disagreed with Plato or Avicenna. But he agreed with them that metaphysical truth was timeless. Were the angelic doctor alive today, he would no doubt argue against Descartes, Kant and Hegel. But such an argument across the ages would itself presuppose the common conviction that metaphysical truth is independent of any age.[5]

But it is a most disturbing fact that what has never been questioned by metaphysi-

5. For a contemporary example of metaphysical argument across the ages in St. Thomas' behalf, cf. E. Gilson, *Being and Some Philosophers* (Toronto: Pontifical Institute of Mediaeval Studies, 1949).

cians before has been questioned by metaphysicians since the middle of the nineteenth century. For the first time, the view
has come to be entertained that metaphysical truth, far from transcending history, is
on the contrary essentially tied to it. And
this suggests the possibility of a revolution
in metaphysics, more radical than any
other ever attempted. When a past metaphysician denied the existence of God he
still clung to the idea of timeless metaphysical truth. This idea was itself denied
when Nietzsche asserted that God is dead.[6]

6. Cf. especially *The Joyful Wisdom,* #125. Cf.
M. Heidegger, "Nietzsche's Wort 'Gott is tot,'"
Holzwege (Frankfurt: Vittorio Klostermann,
1950), p. 222: "Der Name Wahrheit bedeutet
jetzt weder die Unverborgenheit des Seienden,
noch die Uebereinstimmung einer Erkenntnis mit
dem Gegenstand, noch die Gewissheit als das
einsichtige Zu — und Sicherstellen des Vorgestell-
ten. Wahrheit ist jetzt, und zwar in einer wesens-
geschichtlichen Herkunft aus den genannten
Weisen ihres Wesens, die bestaendigende Be-
standsicherung des Umkreises, aus dem her der
Wille zur Macht sich selbst will." We cannot
agree that truth, for Nietzsche, is "will-to-power
willing itself." Rather, it would seem to be will-
to-power willing something *beyond* itself which
will itself creates. Even so, Heidegger clearly sees

R. G. Collingwood said nothing new when he affirmed that metaphysical presuppositions are unprovable. But that the validity of these presuppositions depends on their historical setting was a revolutionary assertion on his part.[7] Nor are Nietzsche and Collingwood isolated examples. Among others who would historicize metaphysical truth are metaphysicians as diverse as Dilthey and Croce, Dewey and Heidegger.[8]

not only that but also how Nietzsche historicizes metaphysical truth.

In these notes, we have made no attempt to be consistent as regards citation of German passages. When easily translatable or available in good translations, we have given them in English. Otherwise we have preferred to give the original.

7.   Cf. *An Eassay on Metaphysics* (Oxford: Clarendon Press, 1940). Cf., however, *infra* note 33.

8.   For Dilthey, cf., e.g., *Briefwechsel Zwischen Wilhelm Dilthey und dem Grafen Paul York von Wartenburg, 1877-1897* (Halle: Max Niemeyer, 1923), (e.g., York's statement, p. 251: "Hence there is no genuine philosophizing which is not historical. The distinction between systematic philosophy and history of philosophy is in principle false"). On Dilthey and York, cf. Heidegger, *Sein und Zeit* (Halle: Max Niemeyer, 1935), pp. 397 ff. For Croce, cf. his *History as the Story of Liberty* (New York: Allen and Unwin,

What is it that metaphysicians of such divergent viewpoints have in common?

If metaphysical truth is timeless, then man, the animal capable of recognizing this truth, must have a capacity which is itself timeless. This is an implication which traditional metaphysicians could easily accept; for they believed in a human nature which, though subject to accidental historical changes, was essentially permanent. But what if there is no such thing as a permanent human nature? What if the distinction between permanent nature and historical change is a false distinction: if man's very being is historical? All the metaphysicians just referred to, and many more, have rejected the doctrine of human nature, and have replaced it with what may be called a doctrine of historicity. And as a result they have been forced to ask whether perhaps just as human being

1941). For Dewey, cf. his doctrine, appearing in many of his works, of a natural and a social matrix, constituting a situation limiting all human activities, philosophy included. For Heidegger, cf. *infra* note 44.

changes throughout history so must metaphysical truth. If man's very being is inseparable from his history, must the same not be true of his grasp of metaphysical truth? And must not then what is metaphysically true in one period of history differ from what is metaphysically true in another? Clearly, the doctrine of historicity is a weighty doctrine, not only in itself but also because of the questions it raises for metaphysics as a whole.

But it is a doctrine difficult to cope with. It cannot, for example, be regarded as obviously true because proved by empirical history. History may show that man is subject to historical change; it does not prove that his very being is involved in this change. The doctrine of historicity is not an empirical generalization but a metaphysical thesis.[9]

9. Thus Dilthey's statement "only history brings to light the potentialities of human being *(Dasein)*" *(Schriften,* V, [Berlin and Leipzig: B. G. Teubner, 1924], p. xci) is a metaphysical thesis, not an empirical generalization. Any Aristotelian would agree that potentialities are disclosed only by their actualization. But he would not concede

Nor can this metaphysical thesis be regarded as obviously false. One cannot, for example, fall straightway to refuting it, in

that our knowledge of essential human potentialities is subject to perpetual revision as history causes new actualities to come into view; nor would the study of history extract this admission from him. Conceivably man's essential potentialities have long been disclosed; and if subsequent history *does* bring novel potentialities to light, it is because man has unessential as well as essential potentialities, and because his essential potentialities can be perverted in countless ways. On Dilthey's views on human nature and human history, cf. Collingwood *The Idea of History* (Oxford: Clarendon Press, 1946), pp. 171 ff.

Karl Loewith has made this astute observation: "Die historischen Abwandlungen der vielfachen Interpretationen des Menschseins. . . . beweisen nicht, dass sich die menschliche Natur je wesentlich geaendert haette; sie verweisen nur auf einen Wandel im Selbstverstaendnis des Menschen. Sowenig es eine moderne Natur gibt, wohl aber eine moderne Naturwissenschaft, sowenig gibt es eine moderne Menschennatur und insofern einen 'modernen Menschen,' wohl aber zeitgemaesse und antiquierte Anthropologie." (*Wesen und Wirklichkeit des Menschen, Festschrift fuer H. Plessner* (ed.) K. Ziegler, [Goettingen: Vandenhoeck and Ruprecht, 1957], p. 64). Loewith's distinction serves to corroborate our point that empirical history does not, by itself, suffice to establish the doctrine of historicity. On the terms of such traditional concepts as substance and nature. For the doctrine of historicity is unintelligible in these terms and indeed implies their falsehood. Before the metaphysician asks whether or not the doctrine of historicity is true he must be sure to have understood it in the terms it requires. But such an understanding is a subtle and complex task.[10]

other hand, his distinction does not, by itself, refute the doctrine of historicity. If there is a human nature, then the historical changes of human self-understanding are as irrelevant to that nature as are the changes in the physical sciences to physical nature. But if human being is an historically situated self-making, then the historical changes in human self-understanding (itself a form of human self-making) must necessarily affect human being.

On the point made in this note, cf. also *infra* note 34.

10. As a rule, non-metaphysicians cannot even recognize this task, let alone perform it. The psychologist W. McDougall writes: "The impossibility of banishing altogether the notion of substance is even clearer in the case of psychological than of physical science. My consciousness is a stream of consciousness which has a certain unique unity; it is a multiplicity of distinguishable parts or features which, although

For this reason, we wish in this lecture to inquire into the meaning of the doctrine of historicity only, and to suspend judgment as to its truth or falsehood. Our inquiry into its meaning will proceed in two stages. We shall first seek to elicit the metaphysical assumptions without which the doctrine of historicity cannot arise, and then seek to state the principal metaphysical categories without which it cannot be maintained. The first effort is to ensure that we understand the doctrine in terms proper to it; the second, to give an understanding of the doctrine itself. But the question which concerns us most of all will be dealt with in the context of the second effort: whether the doctrine of historicity necessitates the surrender of the age-old idea of timeless metaphysical truth.

they are perpetually changing, yet hang together as a continuous whole within which the change goes on." (*Body and Mind*, [London: Methuen, 1911], p. 162). What "unique unity" or "hanging together" must be accounted for, and how does "substance" account for it? Is "substance" the source of identity? And is *self*-identity a mere species of the genus identity?

THE PRESUPPOSITIONS OF THE
DOCTRINE OF HISTORICITY

Our inquiry into metaphysical presuppositions, like any such inquiry, is apt to arrive at unfamiliar or even abstruse terms. It is therefore prudent to set out with terms which are familiar, and close to common sense.

One such set of terms is furnished by a well-known distinction made by R. G. Collingwood. History consists of actions performed by man, not of natural events which happen to him; and the latter are historical only by virtue of their relation—potential or actual—to the former. Caesar's decision at the Rubicon, or Napoleon's fate at Waterloo, are historical primarily. An eruption of Mount Vesuvius or an earthquake in San Francisco are part of history only secondarily, because they are a challenge to human action. And if they occurred on a star on which no men live they would not be part of history at all.

Collingwood's distinction, though complex, may for the present purpose be expounded with the utmost brevity. A natural event has an "outside" only. An historical action has an "inside" as well as an outside. The outside consists of physical bodies and their movement. The inside consists of human thoughts—aims, plans and decisions. Once the historian has described both the outside and the inside of an action he need no longer inquire why what happened did happen. He has already explained why Caesar crossed the Rubicon if he has correctly described Caesar's ambitions, his appraisal of the political situation and his eventual decision.[11]

This distinction between natural event and historical action is an assumption, although one which most men would be willing to make—in practice if not in theory. But the assumption is not that there are conscious human beings who believe themselves to be planning, deciding, and performing actions. This is a plain and indisputable fact. The assumption is that on at least some occasions the belief of these

11.   Collingwood, *The Idea of History*, pp. 213 ff. *et passim.*

agents is a correct belief; that is, that there are occasions when the categories in which the planning, deciding and performing agents understand their behavior are the categories in which it must be understood. Men are not invariably subject to compulsive urges when they believe themselves to be making free decisions. Not all imagined acting for reasons is in fact irrational behavior productive of rationalizations. In short, there is free action, not merely the appearance of free action. This, very briefly and very broadly, is the first assumption.[12]

No doubt it gives rise to baffling questions. Can individuals alone act, or groups as well as individuals? Is all acting rational,

12.   It is an assumption because it can, with some plausibility, be denied. Positivists will seek to explain the sequence "x entertains an objective," "x decides upon an action calculated to realize this objective," and "x performs the action," in terms of laws which cover this sequence, rather than in terms of x's own categories which involve no reference to such laws. At the same time, the assumption of free action is one which manifestly even a positivist will make in practice, i.e., while he himself is the deciding and acting x.

or is there irrational as well as rational
acting? Does historical action include its
consequences, and if so, unintended as
well as intended ones? Finally, is the division between natural event and human action an exhaustive division? Or can there
be occurrences which are neither? This
last question would have been vital to any
Jew standing at the foot of Mount Sinai,
and to any Christian standing at the foot
of the Cross. But such is the secularism of
the present age that it is often forgotten.[13]

13. It is not, however, forgotten by all modern
     philosophers of history. Among those who re-
     member it are Schelling and Heidegger.
         Does belief in divine action in history *ipso
     facto* commit the believer to the doctrine of
     historicity? The study of mediaeval philosophy
     shows that this is far from the case. A thinker
     such as St. Augustine, though believing that
     "the fundamental principle for the pursuit of this
     religion (i.e., Christianity) is history" (*De Vera
     Religione* VII, 3), can nevertheless credit pagan
     Platonists with having perceived *some* truth. And
     a thinker such as St. Thomas Aquinas, while
     maintaining that revealed doctrine is the highest
     truth, nevertheless insists that unaided philo-
     sophical effort can achieve *some* knowledge
     (*Summa Theologica* I, q. 1 a. 1). Both thinkers
     affirm a human nature which, however affected

But there is no need here to raise such baffling questions. It suffices to stress that if the doctrine of historicity is to be maintained, a qualitative distinction between nature and history must somehow and somewhere be drawn. For if it is not drawn, history reduces itself to a mere species of natural process, different from other kinds only in that it happens in or to man. To draw this distinction adequately, the terms "natural event" and "human action" may not suffice. But they are certainly both obvious and indispensable.[14]

by the fall, on the one hand, by divine salvation on the other, nevertheless *is* a nature.

14.   Divine action in history, as understood in the Bible, does not rule out freedom. Thus God's use of Nebuchadnezzar for His purposes does not rule out the reality of Nebuchadnezzar's own purposes which are, to be sure, very different from those of God. Further, the divine purpose in this case—the meting out of just punishment —presupposes freedom on the part of those who are to be punished.

In the context of secularistic interpretations of history, human freedom is sometimes denied because of the "well-known fact that in history the results of our willed actions reach beyond the mark of their intended goal, thus revealing

But by itself, an ontological distinction between natural event and historical action does not justify the doctrine of historicity. As we have said, this is an as-

an inner logic which overrules the will of man" (Frank, *op. cit.*, p. 137). The fact here referred to is real enough. But it does not prove (and Frank does not think it proves) the unreality of human freedom: that history is sheer fate. It suggests, on the contrary (as Hegel, for example, well knew), that freedom in history is real enough to give rise to the most momentous consequences; although, because human freedom is finite, these consequences are always partly, and often wholly, other than those intended. History is never fate. But it is true enough that history often *looks* like fate: when the consequences of human acting have become at once so powerful and so alien to human purposes as to seem to leave, or even in fact to leave, men wholly at their mercy. When this happens history assumes a degree of tragedy which no vain fight against nature can ever match. The latter is merely contradiction. In history there is self-contradiction: when the circumstances in which men find themselves—alien, unwilled, and even heroically though vainly fought against—are nevertheless the product of human action. Tragic self-contradiction in history reaches its climax when the alien and unwilled consequences flow from the actions of the same men who later vainly fight against them, shaken to the core by the monstrous consequences of their actions.

sumption which most men would be willing to make. But few of these would accept the doctrine of historicity. For it is
one thing to admit that men are capable
of free action, and hence of a history. It is
another thing altogether to assert that man
—the being capable of a history—is himself
the product of history. Indeed, conceivably those making the first assertion might
reject the second as incompatible with it.
Is it not the case that man, if capable of
free action and hence of a history, must
have a nature unalterably endowed with
this capacity: a nature, that is, which is
radically non-historical?

If this is indeed the case, then the doctrine of historicity must be false, and history as a whole can be of no interest for
ontology. For ontology is concerned with
being *qua* being, and hence with human
being *qua* being and *qua* human. But this
concern includes only the capacity for free
action, and hence for history, not the actual and accidental uses made of it. If the
doctrine of historicity is false, then these
latter must be the exclusive concern of the

historian. But history, Aristotle says, is less philosophical even than poetry.[15]

The doctrine of historicity, then, requires a second assumption; and this, like the first, may be stated in familiar if not altogether common-sense terms. There are no permanent natures, distinct from the processes in which they are involved; or at any rate, there is no permanent human nature. This assumption, made familiar by modern "process-philosophers," was well summarized by Samuel Alexander.[16] Process is productive, not merely of new examples in accordance with patterns, but of new patterns as well as of new examples. There is not only change in accordance with laws. There is also a change of laws themselves. Reality as a whole is an historical process. Only if this assumption is made can man's very being be considered historical. Only then can the ontological

15. *Poetics,* Chap. IX, 1451 b 6.
16. S. Alexander, "The Historicity of Things," in *Philosophy and History: Essays presented to Ernst Cassirer,* eds. Paton and Klibanski, (Oxford: Clarendon Press, 1936), pp. 11 ff.

inquiry into what man is reduce itself to an historical inquiry into what he has become.

But while necessary, this assumption, by itself and divorced from the first assumption, is not sufficient for the doctrine of historicity. It implies, to be sure, that the processes which constitute human beings are historical as well as natural. But it also implies that the historical is not qualitatively distinct from the natural. If all reality is an historical process, and is so for the same reason, then the processes which make man what he is are in the end all natural.

In the essay already referred to, Alexander speaks of the historicity of *all* things. There is history, he holds, wherever there is novelty and creativity. But Collingwood rightly protests against the implications of such usage.[17] The term "historical" ought surely to be reserved for determining acts rather than incompletely determined events; for free decisions made by

17. *The Idea of History*, pp. 210 ff.

man rather than processes—even "creative" ones—which occur in him. Or at any rate, if such a qualitative distinction is not made, then the doctrine of historicity reduces itself to nothing more than the ancient doctrine of a Heraclitean flux, which encompasses man along with all else.

The doctrine of historicity, then, requires the two above assumptions, taken in conjunction. (a) History is qualitatively distinct from nature because there are actions performed by man, as well as events which happen to him or in him; and (b) the distinction between human being and human acting cannot in the end be maintained. Man is not endowed with a permanent nature capable of acting. His "nature" is itself the product of his acting, and hence not a proper nature at all. *In acting, man makes or constitutes himself.*

To assert this is not to deny that man is largely the product of natural processes. Nor is it even to deny that he is the product of divine creation, or subject to divine influence after creation. But it is to assert that, apart from history, man's very being, *qua* being and *qua* human, is deficient. Man is what he becomes and has become; and the processes of becoming which make him distinctively human are historical. But what makes history distinctively historical is human action.

Human being, then, is a self-making or self-constituting process: this emerges as the crucial assumption without which the doctrine of historicity cannot arise. This assumption alone can explain why the ontologist, inquiring into human being *qua* being and *qua* human, should turn historian: whether speculative historian in the fashion of Hegel, or historian pure and simple in the fashion of Croce and Collingwood. For if human being is indeed a self-constituting process, then the ontological study of man cannot be divorced from the study of human history. Divorced from history, it would arrive not at a determinate human nature but at a mere abstract and empty possibility; or, if arriving at a determinate human nature, it would mistake for a permanent nature what is in fact a specific historical product.[18]

THE CONCEPT OF SELF-MAKING

We have now accomplished our first task—the identification of the assumptions without which the doctrine of historicity cannot arise. But we may well wonder how to proceed with the second task—the understanding of the doctrine itself. Is a self-making process intelligible? If not, how can we determine the categories required by the kind of self-making process which is historical? To ask these questions, one need not share the fashionable fear of taking leave of ordinary language even in metaphysical discourse. Any metaphysician who soars boldly above ordinary language might well ask them. Was Schopenhauer right, when he asserted that a *causa sui* is no less absurd than the story of Baron

18. In the above pp. 17-28, "human being is a self-constituting process" has merely been identified as the hypothesis without which the doctrine of historicity cannot arise. For a sketch of the reasons which have made philosophers accept that hypothesis, cf. *infra* pp. 91-99.

von Muenchhausen, who claimed that, having fallen into a swamp, he pulled himself out by his hair?[19]

But here we must remember a warning given earlier in this lecture. A metaphysical doctrine may well seem unintelligible, and yet in fact be unintelligible only in terms of a metaphysics which is its rival. One does well to suspect that this is so in the present case. For the concept of self-making occurs not only in a relatively brief period of modern metaphysics. It is basic to a whole metaphysical tradition which rivals the major Western tradition in metaphysics. The major tradition asserts that *operatio sequitur esse*. But there is also a minor tradition which asserts that, at least in the case of God, *esse sequitur operationem*. This tradition harks back possibly as far as to John Scotus Eriugena and, passing through such thinkers as Jacob Boehme and Schelling, finds a contemporary representative in Nicolas Berdyaev. In the major tradition, God is understood as Pure

19. *Ueber die Vierfache Wurzel des Satzes vom Zureichenden Grunde*, Chap. 2 #8.

Being, and in substantial strains of that
tradition, as creating the world *ex nihilo*.
In the minor tradition, God is understood
as Pure Freedom who, in creating *ex nihilo*,
Himself passes *ex nihilo in aliquid*. The
major tradition is ontological, in the strict-
est sense. The minor tradition would strict-
ly have to be called meontological.[20]

20. For the principle *operatio sequitur esse,* cf.,
     e.g., St. Thomas Aquinas, *Summa Theologica* I,
     q. 75 (which, treating of the human soul, treats
     first "ea quae pertinent ad essentiam animae,"
     then "ea quae pertinent ad virtutem sive potentias
     eius," and finally "ea quae pertinent ad opera-
     tionem eius,") and *Summa Contra Gentiles* II, 21
     and III, 42 ("sicut enim operatio substantiam
     sequitur, ita operationis perfectio perfectionem
     substantiae").

       For the principle *esse sequitur operationem*
     one can cite only with hesitation John Scotus
     Eriugena, *De Divisione Naturae* I, 72 ("Deus
     ergo non erat, priusquam omnia faceret"; "cum
     audimus Deum omnia facere nihil aliud debemus
     intelligere quam Deum in omnibus esse, hoc est,
     essentiam omnium subsistere"). But one can cite
     without any hesitation Jacob Boehme, *Werke,* ed.
     K. W. Schiebler, (Leipzig: Johann Ambrosius
     Barth, 1831-1846), IV, 429 ("Die Freiheit, als
     das Nichts, hat in sich selber kein Wesen") and
     VI, 413 ("Der Ungrund ist ein ewig Nichts, und
     machet aber einen ewigen Anfang, als eine Sucht;
     denn das Nichts ist eine Sucht nach Etwas; . . .

The God of meontological metaphysics would have to be described as a process which (a) because it is pure *making* proceeds from the indifference of sheer possi-

die Sucht ist selber das Geben dessen, das doch auch nichts ist als bloss eine begehrende Sucht"); Schelling, *On Human Freedom*, trans. Gutmann, (Chicago: The Open Court Publishing Company, 1936); and Berdyaev (for Boehme as well as Berdyaev himself), "Jacob Boehmes Lehre von Ungrund und Freiheit," *Blaetter fuer Deutsche Philosophie*, (1932-1933), vol. VI, (especially p. 325: "Boehme hat vielleicht als erster in der Geschichte des menschlichen Denkens erkannt, dass die Grundlage des Seins und vor dem Sein die grundlose Freiheit ist, die leidenschaftliche Begierde des Nichts, zum Etwas zu werden"), and also *The Beginning and the End* (New York: Harper Torchbooks, 1957). Cf. also Hegel, *Logic*, trans. Wallace (London: Geoffrey Cumberlege: Oxford University Press, 1904), #87: "The supreme form of Nought as a separate principle would be Freedom." For Schelling's use of the term μὴ ὄν, as distinct from οὐκ ὄν, cf. *Werke*, (Stuttgart and Augsburg: Cotta Verlag, 1856-1861), II.1, pp. 288 ff., 306 ff.

If the doctrine of the four causes is granted, then St. Thomas' argument against a *causa sui* as required by meontological metaphysics is incontrovertible, cf. *Summa Theologica* I, q. 2, a. 3: "nec . . . invenitur, nec est possibile quod aliquid sit causa efficiens sui ipsius; quia esset prius seipso, quod est impossibile." But can meontological bility of nothingness (μὴ ὄν) into the differentiation of actuality—*ex nihilo in aliquid;* (b) because it is *self*-making establishes its own identity throughout this process by returning upon itself; or, otherwise put, proceeds into otherness, yet cancels this otherness and in so doing establishes itself; (c) because it is *absolute* self-making, actualizes *ex nihilo* the totality of possibilities.

Is such a description illogical or unintelligible? It is unintelligible, to be sure, in terms of a logic which, consisting of a simple forward movement, leaves its terms static and unchanged. But to dismiss the doctrine for this reason alone would be to regard logic—one particular logic—as a wholly autonomous court of appeal in matters metaphysical. But what if every logic and hence this logic is itself metaphysi-

---

metaphysics grant the doctrine of the four causes? The cited passages suffice to show that its *Nihil* must be at once material and efficient cause, and be creative of the formal and final, all of which is, in terms of the doctrine of the four causes, unintelligible.

cally grounded? In that case, it might well be that meontological metaphysics generates a logic of its own, and it is in terms of this logic that it would then have to be understood. And a final judgment as to truth and falsehood would then have to be made, not in terms of one logic arbitrarily taken as absolute standard, but through a confrontation of the conflicting metaphysics themselves.[21]

The above description of the meontological concept of God, however sketchy, suffices to show that it does indeed generate a logic of its own. Its terms alter as the movement proceeds; and they alter because the movement is backward as well as forward: that is, circular. And the logical movement must be of this kind because the real process it describes is a self-constituting process which, in moving forward, integrates and re-integrates its own past into the forward movement.

21. We do not deny, of course, that *some* "metaphysical assertions" are radically unintelligible, and hence neither metaphysical nor assertions.

We cannot here further describe this kind of logic.[22] But we shall henceforth be compelled to use it. We shall be so compelled, that is, if we wish to understand the doctrine of historicity, rather than pass judgment on it before it is understood.

ETERNITY, TEMPORALITY, HISTORICITY

Only a self-constituting process can be in its ontological constitution historical. But not every such process is necessarily historical. This may be shown by a renewed consideration of the meontological concept of God.

This concept signifies a process which is at least quasi-historical, because first its moment of *nihil* must be distinguished from its moment of *aliquid,* and because secondly the moments of *nihil* and *aliquid* constitute themselves into an identity. If there were no distinguishable moments there would be no process at all; and if they did not constitute themselves into an

22. It may be observed in passing, however, that the greatest attempt to explicate this kind of logic is beyond all doubt Hegel's work by that name.

identity the process would be merely temporal.

But while *at least* quasi-historical, this process can also be *no more than* quasi-historical. This is because it must wholly transcend temporality. For while, because it is a self-making, it appropriates the past into presentness, because it is absolute, it appropriates the past absolutely and without remainder. And while, because it is a self-making, it anticipates the future as possibility, because it is absolute, its anticipating of possibility is indistinguishable from its production of actuality. Indeed, it is senseless to speak here of either anticipating or possibility. Absolute or divine self-making, then, is only quasi-historical because it is eternal, or wholly present, a process symbolizable only as circular: for it is an absolute returning upon itself.[23]

23. Cf., e.g., Hegel, *Werke*, (Berlin: Duncker and Humblot, 1847), VII. 1, p. 60: "Im positiven Sinne der Zeit kann man . . . sagen: Nur die Gegenwart ist, Das Vor und Nach ist nicht; aber die concrete Gegenwart ist das Resultat der Vergangenheit, und sie ist traechtig mit der Zukunft. Die wahre Gegenwart ist somit die Ewigkeit."

And yet this eternity *is* quasi-historical. Something really goes on. Its end is, and yet is not, identical with its beginning.[24]

24. What distinguishes the meontological concept of eternity from that of such thinkers as Boethius (*De Consolatione Philosophiae* V: "nunc stans," "interminabilis vitae tota simul et perfecta possessio") and Plotinus (*Enneads* III, 7.3: ζωὴ μένουσα ἐν τῷ αὐτῷ ἀεὶ παρὸν τὸ πᾶν ἔχουσα," "a life remaining in sameness, always possessing the whole as present") is that here *direction,* even though sublated in eternity, is also preserved in it. Thus Schelling can describe eternity as a "self-renewing movement" (*Werke,* I. 8, p. 230, trans. Bolman, *The Ages of the World,* [New York: Columbia University Press, 1942], p. 116). Thus also the Hegelian Idea, at the end of the *Logic,* is a return to Being, which is at its beginning; and yet the process from Being to Idea has a direction which remains preserved. And Hegelian Absolute Spirit, arising after and on the basis of both Nature and History, is a return to the realm of Logic which is prior to both Nature and History; and yet in this return both Nature and History are preserved.

It ought to be added, however, that Hegel's synthesis of history and eternity caused a split among his followers between "left-wingers" who retained historical direction but abandoned eternity, and "right-wingers" who retained eternity but abandoned historical direction; and that this split among Hegelians has remained until this day. The most fascinating contemporary "left-

To identify historicity proper, then, it
will be necessary to distinguish it from
mere temporality. But it will also be necessary to distinguish it from the quasi-
historicity of eternity. And it will be seen
that the concept of self-making marks historicity off from mere temporality; but that
to mark it off from quasi-historical eternity
another concept is needed, second in importance for the doctrine of historicity only
to that of self-making itself. This is the
concept of *situation*. Only a being which is
a self-making-in-a-situation can be, in its
ontological constitution, historical.

First, historicity differs from mere tem-

wing" and "right-wing" interpretations are, re-
spectively, Alexandre Kojève, *Introduction à la
Lecture de Hegel* (Paris: Gallimard, 1947), and
I. Iljin, *Die Philosophie Hegels als Kontemplative
Gotteslehre* (Bern: A. Francke Ag., 1946). Cf.
also *infra* note 41.

Dissatisfied with the Hegelian synthesis,
Schelling in his old age produced a profound and
revolutionary synthesis of his own. But signifi-
cantly, Schelling's synthesis remained a fragment.
Cf. *The Ages of the World* and my article, "Schelling's Concept of Positive Philosophy," *The Review of Metaphysics*, VII, (1954), 563 ff.

porality. The temporal past survives in the present only as the present effect of past events. This is true even if the past is remembered, provided memory is regarded, not as a present act of recollection, but as a mere event to be understood solely in terms of past events. The past is historical only if, and to the extent that, it is capable of present appropriation and re-enactment. And human being is *qua* being historical only if such acts enter into its ontological constitution. If man has a permanent nature, then he may no doubt have an historical past; but his nature is not for that reason historical. But if man is a self-constituting process then the historical past must enter into his present being. For this process can constitute and re-constitute itself only if it appropriates and re-appropriates at least some of the past.

Again, the historical differs from the merely temporal future. The temporal future is present only in this sense, that the present is pregnant with but limited possibilities. This is true even if the future is feared or hoped for, provided fear and hope are understood as mere present effects of past events. The historical future is presently appropriated as anticipation. All free acting involves an anticipating, a projecting-into-future. Hence, if there is such a thing as free acting at all, there is also an historical as distinct from a merely temporal future. But only if human being is a self-making does this future enter into its present ontological constitution.[25]

25. Both Collingwood and Heidegger recognize that the historical past is truly historical only because it can be appropriated and re-enacted in the present. But whereas Collingwood, concentrating attention on the epistemology of historiography, seems to regard such a re-enactment as mostly, if not entirely, an affair of the present historian, Heidegger considers all such re-enactment of the past to be mediated by the anticipating of the future which is cast back on the past. Cf., e.g., *Einfuehrung in die Metaphysik*, (Tuebingen: Max Niemeyer, 1953), p. 34: "Geschichte als Geschehen ist das aus der Zukunft bestimmte, das Gewesene uebernehmende Hindurchhandeln und Hindurchleiden durch die Gegenwart." Cf. also *Sein und Zeit*, especially #74. While it is not necessary for the present purpose to enter into a discussion of this issue, it may be said in passing that of the two, Heidegger's would appear to be

Thus, finally, the historical differs from the merely temporal present. The temporal present is a vanishing point of passage. The historical present is an act of integration in which anticipated future possibilities are integrated with past actualities into present action. If man has a permanent nature, then such acts add up merely to what he *does*. But if his being is a self-making, then they constitute also what he *is*.

So much for the distinction between historicity and temporality. We now turn to the distinction between historicity and quasi-historical eternity. Most generally stated, historical being is historical—rather than quasi-historical and eternal—because its presently appropriated is ontologically distinct from its actual past, and because, in anticipating the future as a possibility, it

the profounder conception, if only because he squarely faces up to what Collingwood notes only occasionally and in passing: that if human being is *qua* being and *qua* human historical, there can be no ontological divorce between the historical consciousness of the historian and the consciousness of the historical agent who is involved in history, and geared to the future.

does not *ipso facto* produce it as actuality.

The presently re-enacted past would differ from the actual past even if everything humanly capable of re-enactment could be re-enacted; that is, if historical consciousness could reproduce the whole historical past without omission or distortion. I cannot physically, but only in my imagination, refight the battle of Waterloo, if only because they who fought it are dead and gone. I cannot literally cope with the San Francisco earthquake, if only because the earthquake is irretrievably past; and if it occurred again it would be a different earthquake. Nor can I , by re-enacting my state of mind at the age of ten, become now ten years of age.

Again, my presently anticipated future would differ from the actual future even if I could anticipate with total accuracy everything capable of anticipation; that is, if I were endowed with the gift of prophetic omniscience. I cannot, by anticipating the actions of future generations, produce either the generations or their actions. Nor can I, by planning for presently predicted future natural catastrophes, produce now these catastrophes and enact my present plans. Indeed, merely by virtue of being planning, all planning is ontologically distinct from acting, and hence involves the distinction between possibility and actuality. Hence all planning is finite, simply by virtue of being planning; and an omniscient being would not plan at all.

Thus, finally, the historical differs from the quasi-historical or eternal present. It is an act of integration which is in principle incomplete. Its return-upon-itself is never absolute, but fragmented by the loss of a past which it cannot recapture, and by the refractoriness of a future which refuses to be subdued into presentness. It is, in short, a returning-upon-self within the limits of a *situation*.

These limits are many and varied in kind. But those thus far referred to are all of the same kind. Historical acts of self-making all occur on the basis and in the context of events which simply *happen,* independently of all acts of self-making; that is, of *natural events.* All historical acting occurs in a *natural situation;* otherwise it would not be historical at all.[26]

Historical being, then, differs in its ontological structure from temporal and eternal being alike. At its lowest, it may lapse into a dream-like flux barely distinct from a merely temporal passage. At its highest, it may rise to actions which make it seem to fall but little short of eternity. But it is only so long as it transcends temporality to some degree that it attains to humanity and historicity; and it is only so long as it does not transcend temporality absolutely —that is, so long as it remains finite—that it remains historical and human.

26.   Idealists such as Schelling and Hegel recognize, as much as any naturalist, that history remains dependent on nature so long as it is history at all. If they disagree with naturalism in this matter, it is in attributing a direction to history, and in claiming that its aim is emancipation from dependence on nature, and hence transcendence of history itself. This view is already contained in one strain of Kantian thought, cf. my article "Kant's Concept of History," *Kant-Studien,* XLVIII (1956-57), 381 ff. Cf. further on this issue, *infra* note 27.

THE CONCEPT OF SITUATION

We must now consider the relation between situation and situated self-making. That relation has a characteristic which is of the greatest importance for the further development of the doctrine of historicity. But it is easily overlooked or explained away.

We have seen that self-making, to be both human and historical, must be finite. But if the situation which situates it were not ontologically other than it, self-making could not be genuinely finite. Its limitations, such as they were, would be subject to possible elimination by acts of self-transcendence. On the other hand, if the situation were *wholly* other than the self-making it situates, then the latter would not be a finite self-making either. It would either be a simple product, and hence not a self-making at all, or else it would be subject only externally to bounds, unaffected by them in its inner structure. In the latter case, it would be finite in one respect, self-making in another. But we have already seen that this is impossible. It is by virtue of its historicity that human self-making is finite; yet only if historicity is permeated in its inner structure by temporality can it be historicity at all.

The relation between situation and situated self-making, then, is a dialectical relation. The situation which situates self-making must be other than it; and it must yet enter into its ontological constitution, thus losing some of its otherness.

This dialectical characteristic is easily ignored or explained away, but with grave consequences. To ignore the aspect of otherness in the situation is to lapse into the kind of idealism which regards all limitation of the self as the self's own self-limitation. And to stress nothing but the aspect of otherness is to lapse into the kind of naturalism for which the self is, in the end, the mere product of its environment.[27] Un-

27. If Fichte's idealism regards the world—the "non-self"—as the self's own self-limitation, however, it is not so much because he ignores or underestimates its aspect of otherness. It is rather because his belief in the absolute ontological primacy of morality leads him to consider the world as the mere "material of our duty rendered

easily between these extremes would rest the attempt to dispose of dialectic by means of a dualistic doctrine, for which the self is, on the one hand, subject to external bounds, and on the other, unaffected by these bounds in its internal self-constitution.

sensuous," (*Werke,* [Berlin: Veit and Company, 1845], V, 185), incapable of giving absolute resistance to the moral will. Dewey, while *qua* metaphysician describing human being as a self-making-in-a-situation, abandons this concept whenever he falls prey to naturalistic or positivistic ways of thinking.

Unlike Fichte, Schelling and Hegel regard the human self as limited by a nature genuinely other-than-self. If they nevertheless arrive at idealistic conclusions, it is because they hold the human self to be capable of transcending, not only dependence on nature but also all finiteness and hence humanity and selfhood itself. If and when such transcendence occurs, natural limitations such as temporality and death still exist, of course; but because they no longer structure the self—itself now more than self—they have become "unessential." Cf. also *infra* note 31.

It is existential philosophy which denies transcendence-of-situation, such as is asserted by Schelling and Hegel; and this denial has brought fully to light the dialectical relation between situation and situated self-making. Cf. further *infra* pp. 71-90.

Such a doctrine might identify the aspects of otherness in the situation with the *actual* limitations which it imposes on self-making, and the aspect of non-otherness with the self's *awareness* of these limitations. And it could point out that the self is subject to natural limitations quite regardless of its awareness of them; but that, once the self *is* aware of them, they have become part of its inner constitution.

But there can be no dualism between self and self-awareness—the former described as a simply passive, the latter as a simply active aspect of self-making. If the self *qua* subject to natural limitations were simply passive it would not—or not yet—be a self at all, since the self is *ex hypothesi* a process of self-making. And if awareness were wholly active, then the self would, in becoming aware of limitations, *ipso facto* transcend them; indeed, there would be no difference between self-awareness and self-images created at random. But the self, *qua* subject to limitations, is already a self and hence not simply passive; and self-awareness *is* self-awareness precisely because it does not, simply by virtue of being awareness, transcend the limitations which it is aware of: hence it is not simply active.

The conclusion then, is clear. If human being is a situated self-making, then the relation between it and the situation which situates it must be dialectical. Finite self-making must be understood as limited by a situation which is other than it, and which still enters into its internal constitution; and nevertheless finite self-making must *be* a self-making, not the mere product of external events. But how this dialectical relation manifests itself depends on the type of situation by which self-making is situated. Yet the only type thus far referred to is the natural situation.

THE CONCEPT OF HISTORICAL SITUATION

But the concepts of self-making and natural situation are not yet sufficient to describe the structure of a being which is *qua* being historical. At least one further concept is needed—that of *historical situation.*

No one can doubt that there are historical situations. The sphere of possible human acting is circumscribed not only by natural events but also by other human actions. To deny this would be to deny the obvious.

The question is not, however, whether there are historical situations but whether they affect man's very being. If man has a permanent nature, then historical situations affect only its accidental manifestations. But if human being is a self-making, then, in affecting the possibilities of human acting, historical situations must affect also the possibilities of human being. The concept of historical situation must be, in that case, an ontological as well as an historical concept.[28]

28. This is the precise reason why Hegel, inquiring into human being *qua* being and *qua* human, must inquire into history; for man *is* what he has *become*, or rather, what he has freely *made* of himself.

It is a commonly held view that Hegel asserted "laws" of history, which imply at once the denial of human freedom and the possibility of predicting the future. But Hegel never made predictions. And he regarded history, not as gov-

If human being is a self-making, then there is need for two concepts of historical situation which are *prima facie* wholly distinct. First, an individual's present possibilities of acting are affected by his own past acting. On the one hand, he can do higher mathematics now because he has done lower mathematics in the past. On the other hand, because he has faced up to grief and sorrow he has lost his childlike innocence. No doubt an individual's past acts of self-making affect his present acts in varying degrees, from the lowest form of subconscious influence to the highest form of conscious recollection. But if human being is a self-making, they must all affect them to some degree. For personal identity is, in that case, nothing but the process which integrates past acts of self-making into present acts; and personality is a history which begins at birth and ends with death.

erned by patterns of recurrence, but as a single plot. Further, his historical dialectic, far from denying human freedom, on the contrary presupposes it. Cf. further *infra* note 34.

But there is need also for a second concept of historical situation, and of the two this indeed is the more obvious. The acting of men is affected by that of other men, as well as by their own. Mozart has created possibilities of experience which but for his work would not exist. And citizenship in a Greek city-state is a possibility lost for men of this century. If man has a permanent nature, then our specific twentieth century situation is irrelevant to that nature and its essential possibilities; and the twentieth century situation concerns only the historian, not the ontologist. But if human being is a self-making, then our twentieth century situation is not irrelevant to the concerns of ontology. In circumscribing what contemporary man can experience and do, that situation, in that case, circumscribes also what contemporary man can be and is.[29]

29.   It is for this reason that man's "present situation," once considered irrelevant for metaphysics, has pre-occupied modern metaphysicians, from Hegel (cf., e.g., the Preface to his *Phenomenology of Mind*, trans. J. B. Baillie, [2d ed.; Allen and Unwin, 1931]) to Jaspers (cf., e.g., his

What is the relation between historical situation and historically situated self-making, in the two senses just described? We have already dealt in general with the dialectical relation between situation and what it situates. What remains to be shown is how this applies to the historical situation.

Here, as everywhere, the situating must remain other than the situated, if the latter is to be situated at all. Still, historical otherness must differ from natural otherness. The natural situation simply limits; and the situated is free toward this limitation only in that it can accept it.[30] But the historically situating cannot simply limit the historically situated; for here the situating and the situated are both human ac-

Man in the Modern Age, [Garden City, N.Y.: Doubleday, 1957]) and Heidegger (cf. virtually all his later writings).

30.   This is true only so long as the natural is artificially isolated from the historical situation—an isolation which is artificial because it nowhere exists. Man-in-civilization obviously transforms nature. But man *qua* civilized is *both* naturally and historically situated. Cf. also *infra* note 32.

tion. Despite this fact, the historically situating must do *some* limiting, if what it
situates is to be situated at all. But because
of this fact, the historically situating augments as well as limits. For the freedom of
the situated toward the situating cannot be
confined to the acceptance of alien limitations. Because the situating and the situated are both human action, the freedom
of the situated extends to the appropriating of aspects of the situating, that is, to
the integrating of these into its own process
of self-constitution. Natural facts such as
lost childhood and present middle age are
limitations which I can only accept. Historical facts such as the work of Mozart can
become part of myself to the extent to
which I can appropriate them. But insofar
as I in fact do so, the historical other at
once loses its otherness and augments my
selfhood.

Unlike the natural situation, then, the
historical situation both limits and augments what it situates; and it is the togeth-
erness of both which alone can constitute
a situation as historical. If the historically

situated could ever appropriate the totality of what situates it historically, it would rise above history.[31] And if the historically situated were ever wholly incapable of appropriating any part of what situates it historically, it would fall below history. In both cases, history would be lost. Every historical situation, then, *qua* historical, is a conjunction of limitation and opportunity; as it were, of fate and freedom.

This conclusion gives rise to another which is no less important. Natural situations fall into types; and if and when they bring forth qualitative novelty it is, so to speak, by accident. But in the case of historical situations, the possibility of novelty

31. According to Schelling and Hegel, such a rise in fact occurs when human being—no longer historical—rises to Absolute Spirit. Reaching this stage it still differs, however, from the quasi-historical eternity of the meontological God. For while the latter is beyond all situatedness the former transcends a situatedness which this transcendence presupposes. Moreover, natural otherness has not vanished, and even historical otherness has not wholly done so; everything that remains other has merely become "unessential." Cf. also *supra* note 27.

is part and parcel of their essential structure. For any free and novel act enlarges the scope of subsequent acting, so long as it remains capable of being appropriated. But if human being is a self-making, this implies that the scope of human being differs from one historical situation to another; that, to the extent to which it is historically situated, man's very humanity differs from age to age.

HISTORICISM

These conclusions give rise to the question with which we began this lecture. The question then was: does the doctrine of historicity imply the surrender of the idea of timeless metaphysical truth? We can now give a more precise formulation: if human being is an historically situated self-making, must all its activities be historically situated—metaphysics included?

Prima facie, the case against the metaphysical claim to timeless truth is overwhelming. First, if human being is a self-making, then metaphysics too must be a form of self-making. In rising to metaphysical knowledge, self-making may or may not be creating the truths to the knowledge of which it rises. But the knowledge itself must, at any rate, be part of the self-making process. And if metaphysical truth is transhistorical, then metaphysical knowledge must be a transhistorical form of self-making.

But secondly, a transhistorical form of self-making seems *prima facie* impossible. If man has a permanent nature, then it may be possible to distinguish between finite capacities and capacities such as that for metaphysical knowledge which transcend finitude. But if human being is a self-making, then such a distinction between aspects which leave each other unaffected is surely untenable. For the self-making process is one in which all aspects are integrated into a single whole; and it is only by virtue of this integration that the self attains to selfhood at all.

Thus the above-made distinctions are subject to qualification. No doubt one must distinguish, as we have distinguished, between the history which is the life of an individual, and the history which is the life of a civilization. But if human being is a self-making this distinction cannot be absolute. For individual self-making integrates into a present unity not only its own past actions but also the effect on it of the acts of others. Thus merely by virtue of living in the twentieth century, an individual is, *qua* individual, different from what he would have been had he lived in another century.

Further, we did undoubtedly well to distinguish between natural and historical situation. But if human being is a self-making, one cannot distinguish absolutely even between these. Who can doubt that at least man's attitude toward his natural limitations differs from one civilization to another? Moreover, bearing in mind the facts of modern technology, who can believe that even man's actual natural limitations are wholly unaffected by history?[32] The

32. Cf. *supra* note 30. It would seem that Fichte was the first to attempt a radical historization of nature, although certain strains in Kant already point in that direction. (Cf. my article, referred

conclusion seems inescapable that, if human being is a self-making, it is *radically* historically situated; that there are no aspects of a man's being which are wholly unaffected by the historical situation in which he exists.

If this is the case, then how can metaphysics be an exception? The metaphysician may claim to be rising above history, to timeless truth. And the metaphysician who regards human being as a self-making

to in note 26.) Kant regards natural inclinations as simply given, and hence as both unalterable and innocent. Fichte, in sharp contrast, regards such inclinations as neither unalterable nor innocent, and hence their gradual elimination through cultural and moral effort as a task to be performed by man in history. Consequently, while both thinkers affirm a *summum bonum,* understood as "the correspondence of the will of a rational being with the idea of an eternally valid will (moral goodness) and correspondence of the things outside us with our will (happiness)"—the formulation is Fichte's, *Werke,* VI, 299—Kant means by the latter correspondence the satisfaction of unalterably given and hence morally innocent inclinations (*Werke,* Prussian Academy edition, [Berlin], V, 107 ff.), while Fichte means their gradual elimination through culture. I intend to deal with the relation between Kant and Fichte on this issue elsewhere.

may try to save this claim by interpreting metaphysics as a transhistorical form of self-making. But if human being is a self-making, must not the transhistorical integrate itself with the historical, and thus itself become infected with historicity? It may seem, then, that the distinction between the historical and the transhistorical, if admissible at all, is only a relative distinction; a distinction, that is, which appears absolute only to a standpoint which is itself historically situated.

This conclusion, if accepted, revolutionizes the very concept of metaphysics. Metaphysics, once regarded as aiming at timeless truth, is now reduced to an activity aiming at what *seems* timeless truth, from the standpoint and within the limits of an historical situation. All metaphysics, that is, is reduced to a sequence of historically relative *Weltanschauungen*.

The consequence of this is that metaphysics is in principle superseded by history. For, on the one hand, the metaphysician—the person who lives by a particular *Weltanschauung*—cannot recognize its historical relativity; for if he did he could no longer live by it. On the other hand, *somebody* must recognize the relativity of all *Weltanschauungen,* and in so doing he passes beyond all metaphysics. This somebody is the historian.

The historian's history of *Weltanschauungen* is, to be sure, forever incomplete in one sense; but it is forever complete in another. It is forever incomplete because, itself written from an historical standpoint, it must be rewritten in every age. But it is forever complete in that it leaves no room, beyond the history of metaphysics, for an independent inquiry into metaphysical truth.[33]

33. This is the position adopted, for example, by Collingwood in *An Essay on Metaphysics.* It is instructive to note, however, that he is much too subtle a thinker simply to remain with that position. Rather he considers the belief that metaphysics consists of historically changing *Weltanschauungen* itself to spring from a metaphysical thesis of a different order; the thesis being that mind changes through history because it is its own self-constituted functions. Cf., e.g., *The Idea of History,* pp. 288, 292, *Speculum Mentis* (Oxford: Clarendon Press, 1924), p. 207. This latter thesis is neither history nor one *Weltan-*

The position thus arrived at its known as historicism. This term has been given many meanings. But only one of these deserves to be called classical. Historicism, in the classical sense, is the position which asserts that all philosophical are superseded by historical questions. It is "the assertion that the fundamental distinction between philosophical and historical questions cannot in the last analysis be maintained."[34]

schauung among others but rather what Germans would call a *Weltanschauungslehre*.

34. Leo Strauss, *What is Political Philosophy?* (Glencoe, Ill.: The Free Press, 1959), p. 57.

Karl Popper has given his private definition of historicism: "the doctrine that there is a developmental law which can be discovered, and upon which predictions regarding the future of mankind can be based." (*The Open Society and Its Enemies* [London: George Routledge and Son Ltd., 1945], p. 7. and elsewhere.) But this is highly confusing. Hegel—supposedly an historicist in Popper's sense—never made predictions; indeed, precisely because he held that man's very being changes in history he could not believe in "laws . . . upon which predictions regarding the future of mankind can be based." On Popper's account of Hegel, cf. W. Kaufmann, "The Hegel Myth and its Method," *The Philosophical Review,*

THE REFUTATION OF HISTORICISM

But historicism is radically and unqualifiedly untenable; and if the doctrine of historicity necessarily led to historicism it would, for that reason alone, be untenable

LX, (1951), 459 ff. and especially pp. 473 ff. On the other hand, a thinker might well be an historicist in Popper's sense precisely because he is not a historicist in the accepted sense—because he considers human being to have enough permanence to justify predictions based on laws.

The reader who agrees that the doctrine of historicity, if developed to a certain point, leads to historicism, may nevertheless wonder whether there are not other roads to historicism. What, for example, of a simple distinction between the natural sciences, understood as disciplines discovering laws, and historiography, understood as a discipline incapable of discovering laws? But a mere insistence on the unpredictable in history is not enough to justify historicism. Why should it be assumed that the historical changes to which man is subject affect him so profoundly as to make tomorrow's philosophical truth unpredictable today? This assumption, as was shown above (note 9), is a metaphysical thesis, not an empirical generalization. And it can be none other than that developed in the course of this lecture. For if human being consists of a permanent human nature we never come anywhere near historicism; and if human being is a simple rather than a self-constituting process, the process in question is not distinctively historical.

as well. History may stand in need of being rewritten in every age. The philosophy which recognizes this truth cannot itself stand in need of being so rewritten. All other acts of human self-making may be historically situated. The one exception must be the act by which self-making recognizes itself as self-making, and as historically situated. But if this exception is impossible, then the whole doctrine collapses in internal contradiction.

Historicism is faced with a dilemma from which there is no escape. Either it renounces all philosophical assumptions (but then it can make no philosophical assertions; it is, in fact, not historicism at all but simply history[35]), or else it insists that philosophical are superseded by historical questions (but then it is committed to philosophical assumptions which are ruled out by the thesis itself). In this lecture, we have endeavoured to outline the ontology which historicism, as a metaphysical position, would seem to require. But this on-

35. Cf. *supra* note 9.

tology implies that historicism must be false.[36]

Thus one of the two questions which we ask in this lecture is answered in what would seem a thoroughly conclusive manner. The doctrine of historicity, far from implying the surrender of the ancient

36. Cf., e.g., Strauss' remarks on Dewey, *op. cit.*, p. 72.

Our above refutation of historicism may seem to differ but slightly, if at all, from the standard refutation of relativism in general. But the difference is, nevertheless, important. Conceivably the standard refutation may be met by a doctrine which asserts that statements such as "all truth is relative" differ in logical type from statements such as "the statement 'all truth is relative' is true." But our above refutation of historicism cannot be met by this doctrine, at least if it is granted that historicism springs from the doctrine of historicity. For historicism asserts, in that case, not only that all metaphysical assertions are historically relative; it adds that this is so because these assertions are part of an historically situated process of self-making. And it is then forced to concede that the assertion "historicism is true" is also part of this process of self-making. But the crux is that both statements, no matter how different in type, must be part of one and the same self-constituting process; and it is precisely this that historicism cannot account for without collapsing in self-contradiction.

claim to timeless metaphysical truth, is on the contrary compelled to re-assert this claim, if it is not, like historicism, to collapse in internal inconsistency. And thus the most dangerous metaphysical assault ever made on the idea of timeless metaphysical truth has failed. And this failure emboldens us to predict that no similar assault will ever succeed. It would be hazardous indeed to predict the metaphysics of the future, or even that there will be a metaphysics in the future. But it would seem wholly safe to predict that, so long as there is metaphysics at all, it cannot abandon the notion of timeless metaphysical truth.

This crucial conclusion has weighty implications for the doctrine of historicity. It implies that that doctrine, in order to be tenable, must after all find room for transhistorical possibilities of self-making. Moreover, such possibilities, once granted in principle, can hardly be confined to philosophy. Can one dismiss Kierkegaard's claim that Christianity, if a possibility at all, must be substantially the same possibility in the nineteenth century that it was in the first? Can one dismiss the possibility of a radical religious conversion?[37] And can one deny that Mozart, were he alive and at work today, would only *per accidens* be a different Mozart? It would be rash indeed to exempt the arts wholly from historicity; and the example of modern art is enough to give even the rashest pause. At the same time, any single work of genius is a living witness testifying that the total historization of the arts is absurd.

37. This is among the chief questions inspiring Kierkegaard's protest against the historicist thinking of his time. Kant, though anticipating historicist thinking in one strain of his thought, in the end repudiates it precisely because it seems to historicize man's free decision, including the decision for a conversion. (In Kant's case, the conversion is moral rather than religious.) Cf. especially *Werke*, VI, 19 ff., *Religion Within the Limits of Reason Alone*, trans. Greene and Hudson, (Chicago: The Open Court Publishing Company, 1934), pp. 15 ff., and my article, "Kant and Radical Evil," *University of Toronto Quarterly*, XXIII, 339 ff. Cf. also the article referred to in note 26.

HEGEL

But what is true of many false but profound metaphysical doctrines is true of
historicism. Refutation is easiest. More difficult is sympathetic understanding. Most
difficult of all is what combines both: a
genuine response to the challenge.[38]

Such a response was given before historicism ever appeared on the scene, in the
philosophy of Hegel. Hegel perceived with
the utmost clarity a truth wholly beyond
the comprehension of historicism. If human being is a self-making, then it must be
composed of both finite or situated and
infinite or non-situated aspects. It must
have finite or situated aspects, for otherwise it would not be human. And it must
have infinite or non-situated aspects, for

38. Such a response can be given only in terms of
    the doctrine of historicity—which understands the
    grounds for historicism—restated in a form which
    both recognizes and avoids the inconsistencies of
    historicism. It is such a response alone which can
    refute historicism *ab intra*. Mere refutations *ab
    extra* may no doubt be sound enough; but they
    do not provide an understanding of the full
    challenge of historicism, a challenge which has
    far deeper roots than historicism, taken by itself.

otherwise it would be incapable of philosophical self-recognition. Hegel further perceived that, if human being is a self-making, its finite and its infinite aspects must, and yet cannot, integrate themselves into a unity. They must do so because self-identity consists of precisely that integration. They cannot do so because neither aspect can reduce itself to the other. If the infinite reduced itself to the finite aspect, the result would be a relapse into historicism. And if the finite reduced itself to the infinite aspect, man would cease to be human. Hegel expressed all this in a single statement, remarkable enough to be considered a key statement in modern metaphysics: "I raise myself in thought to the Absolute . . . thus being infinite consciousness; yet at the same time I am finite consciousness. . . . Both aspects seek each other and flee each other. . . . I am the struggle between them."[39]

39. *Werke*, (Berlin: 1840), XI, 64, *Lectures On the Philosophy of Religion*, trans. Speirs and Sanderson (London: Kegan Paul, Trench, Truebner and Company, 1895), I, 65.

And yet it is a fact that Hegel in the end let go of this struggle. No subsequent existential thinker exceeds Hegel in emphasis on man's human limitations. Nevertheless he ended up asserting the sublation of man's finite in his infinite aspect. To be sure, this assertion, like all of Hegel's assertions, was made for excellent reasons. For if man remains an unresolved struggle must not his finite infect his infinite aspect, thus rendering philosophy impossible?[40] Still, while few definitive judgments have as yet been made on Hegel, one such judgment has long been made, less by subsequent philosophers than by subsequent historical developments. Hegel's own transhistorical synthesis of the historical and the transhistorical was destroyed by

40. Hegel's ultimate sublation of man's finite in his infinite aspect results not only from philosophical considerations such as those here referred to. It also results from his Christian convictions. But this is too complex a matter to be dealt with here.

On whether the doctrine of man-as-unresolved-struggle must in fact lead back to historicism, cf. the whole remainder of this lecture.

the recalcitrance of subsequent history. And the same fate would befall any attempt to bring Hegelianism up-to-date. Indeed, it is only because of this failure on Hegel's part that historicism could appear on the scene even after Hegel himself had refuted it.[41]

41.   There are two opposite attempts to save Hegel's *Philosophy of History*. In the one, stress is laid on Hegel's refusal to predict the future. But this is here taken to include not only future history but also future philosophical interpretations of history. Hegel's work, which concludes with the modest remark "bis hierher ist das Bewusstsein gekommen" (*Werke*, IX, [Berlin: 1848], p. 546), is viewed as an interpretation of history, not from an absolute standpoint but merely from the standpoint of the early nineteenth century. But this interpretation not only leads back to historicism; it is also contrary to Hegel's explicit intentions. For he holds that history manifests a synthesis of political realities and absolute religious truth: a synthesis which his own age had at least in principle achieved.

The opposite attempt to save Hegel's *Philosophy of History* lays proper stress on Hegel's concept of the transhistoricity of religious and philosophical truth. But it views history as essential only so long as religious and philosophical truth are still in the process of development, and no longer once these truths are fully disclosed. But this ignores Hegel's belief that religious truth,

THE CONCEPT OF HUMAN SITUATION

We are thus left with this inescapable conclusion: if the doctrine of historicity is to be maintained, human being must be understood, after all, as the Hegelian struggle between aspects which seek each other and flee each other; and that struggle must remain in principle unresolvable. The aspects must seek each other because human self-identity must be achieved, if not in integration, so at least in the search for integration. And the aspects must flee each other because if they found each other the result would be either a self-refuting historicism or else a Hegelian elevation of man above humanity. If human being is a self-making, then man is not merely accidentally involved in this unresolvable

to be fully actual, must be embodied in history, an embodiment which includes political realities.

Of the two attempts, the second is more defensible. But in order to be tenable, it would have to show that the events of nineteenth and twentieth century history can be understood in the terms in which Hegel understood history until his time. And it is more than doubtful that such an attempt could succeed.

struggle. This struggle then constitutes what man *is*.

This conclusion, we say, is inevitable. But it gives rise to one crucial question: can human being be this struggle and yet be capable of rising to philosophic self-understanding?

This question has received an answer of the utmost profundity, from the existential philosophers of our own time. According to their teaching, human being manifests, in a thousand forms, the unresolvable struggle which is its essence. But one or some of these forms are qualitatively distinct from all the others, because in these human being *recognizes* itself as a struggle which is in principle unresolvable. This recognition must itself be a form of the struggle, for if it rose above it the struggle would not be unresolvable. At the same time, it is a qualitatively unique form because it understands the struggle, in principle and as a whole.

This doctrine implies a revolutionary concept of metaphysical cognition. In other forms of cognition, the knower may assume the standpoint of a detached subject viewing an object or a world of objects. The self-as-struggle which knows itself as struggle cannot adopt such a standpoint. For to do so would be to break up the reality of unresolvable struggle into two pseudo-realities: a subject which, being a detached spectator, is not involved in the struggle; and an object which, being a mere object-*for*-understanding but *qua* object incapable of *self*-understanding, is not involved in the decisive struggle, either. If human being is unresolvable struggle, then it cannot achieve philosophical self-understanding through the kind of cognition achieved by a spectator—a definition given *ab extra*. The definition required must be a *self*-definition; and this can spring only from existential attempts at radical self-transcendence, in which human being, seeking to rise above the unresolvable struggle which is its essence, recognizes its radical limitations by foundering in the attempt.[42]

42. The correlation between "attempt-at-transcendence," "border situation" and "foundering" is

These attempts must be radically individual, made by each person for himself.

fully developed in Jaspers, *Philosophie*, especially pp. 467 ff. Perhaps the best known and most succinct account is Heidegger's "What is Metaphysics?" in *Existence and Being*, trans. Brock, (London: Vision Press, 1949), pp. 353 ff.

Helmut Kuhn has made a useful distinction between "critical" and "social" existentialism, the former emphasizing "crisis" in the attempt at radical self-transcendence, the latter, "social" existential possibilities falling short of radical self-transcendence, such as what Martin Buber calls an I-Thou-relationship. ("Existentialism," in V. Ferm, *A History of Philosophical Systems* [New York: Philosophical Library, 1950], pp. 405 ff.) If in the present context we refer only to "critical" existentialism, it is because the issue under discussion is the possibility of metaphysical transcendence.

It is true that Buber asserts the possibility not only of inter-human but also of human-divine dialogue. But it must be remembered that the latter is beyond the realm of unaided human effort, and possible only by virtue of divine incursions into time and history.

Kuhn's distinction, while useful, cannot be considered absolute. It would seem that, if Buber could not accept the reality of a divine address to man, he too would be driven to the conclusion that man's unaided effort at transcendence culminates in crisis. (Cf. *infra*, note 49) And Kierkegaard is the "father" of both emphases, stressing the foundering of man's unaided attempts at

But the knowledge attained through them is radically universal. For this is not a person's mere knowledge of his personal situation. It is his knowledge that he is both in principle situated and yet able to recognize his situatedness. This knowledge is universal; and the person who has acquired it has risen to philosophical self-understanding.

It follows, then, that existential philosophy must introduce yet another crucial concept into the ontology of human self-making; and this concept, once introduced, surpasses the concepts of natural and historical situation in significance. The new concept is that of *human situation*.[43]

transcendence, and at the same time committed to belief in divine Grace.

43. Only if two points are perpetually kept in mind can the existential concept of human situation be understood. First, it is not an objective fact laid out before a detached knower, but a situation which situates the knower, and which is understood by him as such only when he faces up to it as his own. The human situation is not an anthropological fact. But neither, secondly, is it a mere part of an individual's autobiography. For though discovered by each for himself, the human situation, when recognized as such, is

This concept is additional to those of natural and historical situation. But the human situation is not a source of additional limitations. Rather, it is the ontological ground of both the natural and the historical situation, and is in turn individuated only in these. Correspondingly, the recognition of the human situation cannot be divorced from that of the natural and the historical situation; it is achieved when the natural and the historical situation are understood radically, as specific manifestations of a universal condition. It is the radicalization of the natural and of the historical situation which discloses the human situation.

This radicalization, however, achieves a qualitatively new insight. A person discovers his natural situation when he comes upon such individual limits as his lost

understood to be universally human. Thus death is part of the human situation, and yet distorted when viewed as a mere objective fact. "All men must die" is a mere objectification. The existential truth is "each man must die for himself," when faced up to by an individual as a truth which applies to himself.

childhood, a disease which afflicts him, or the frailties of old age. He discovers his human situation when he sees, in the foundering attempt at radical self-trans-cendence, that temporality and mortality are universally part of the human lot. Again, a person discovers his historical sit-uation when he faces up, say, to the unique historical limitations and opportunities of the nuclear age. He comes upon his hu-man situation when he recognizes that all history is a conjunction of compulsion and freedom, and that to be subject to the one and to be challenged to realize the other is universally part of the human condition.[44]

44. Heidegger explicitly repudiates historicism (*Sein und Zeit,* p. 396), by means of achieving a radical grasp of historicity, as characterizing the human situation—a step in part anticipated by Dilthey who writes: "das historische Bewusst-sein von der Endlichkeit jeder geschichtlichen Erscheinung . . ., von der Relativitaet jeder Art von Glauben ist der letzte Schritt zur Befreiung des Menschen zu seiner Souveraenitaet" (*Schrif-ten,* VII, [1927], p. 290).

It is a noteworthy fact that in his later works Heidegger becomes once more involved in his-toricism, at a deeper level. Thus in *Was ist das— die Philosophie?* (Pfullingen: Güenther Neske,

Thus the human situation manifests itself only in the natural and the historical
situation, and is yet irreducible to them.

1956), he makes these assertions: (1) philosophy
is wholly bound up with language, and language
is historical; (2) philosophy is essentially Greek,
and hence the term "European philosophy" is a
mere tautology; (3) not only philosophy but
also Heidegger's own inquiry into it is historical;
(4) the identity of philosophy is not that of a
timeless, transhistorical essence but merely an
identity of continuity over a limited period, albeit
one long enough to have lasted from Plato to
Nietzsche; (5) hence every philosophical inquiry
into the "essence" of philosophy can be no more
than a confrontation between two ages. Otto
Poegeler comments as follows (in *Philosophischer
Literaturanzeiger*, XII, [1959], 194 ff.): *Sein und
Zeit* had described *Existenzialien*, or the structure
of human existence, but it had left unanswered
whether or not these *Existenzialien* are universal
categories. For in that work human existence had
been understood only preliminarily; its ultimate
understanding was to be achieved in terms of
Being which was as yet not understood. But
Heidegger's later works do seek to understand
Being, and they understand it historically. That
is, Being is understood as manifesting itself differently in different periods of *Seinsgeschichte*.
Consequently, the *Existenzialien* which structure
human existence must, in the end, be understood
historically as well.

But we must insist that while many—in particular, theologians—might sympathize with the thesis

And the recognition of the human situation occurs only in and through that of the natural and the historical situation; yet it achieves a universality which marks it off

"Being manifests itself differently in different periods," the *total* historization of philosophy toward which the later Heidegger seems to be moving is open to the same objections as the crudest forms of historicism. The very thesis "Being manifests itself differently in different periods" cannot without self-contradiction be historicized.

It is noteworthy in this connection that, like Nietzsche before him, the later Heidegger seems to take refuge more and more in poetry. But such a refuge is surely an escape from the responsibilities proper to philosophy. *Qua* poet, Nietzsche may be entitled to proclaim that "God is dead." But why should anyone accept this proclamation even if he is moved by Nietzsche's poetry and shares his sense of alienation? Why should he not instead lament, with the Psalmist, that "God hides His face"? In the total absence of philosophical argument, the choice is made entirely on authority. But while philosophy assuredly cannot remove this need for choice it cannot escape from its own responsibilities by becoming itself an authority. At least part of the task of philosophy—existential philosophy included—must consist of argument, however inconclusive, such as the systematic elaboration of presuppositions and implications.

On the role of speculative discourse in existential philosophy, cf. further *infra* note 53.

from these latter forms of knowledge. It is the very acceptance of a particular and indeed unique limitation, whether natural or historical, which achieves philosophical universality in the moment of radical anxiety in which a man, recognizing his ultimate finiteness and yet bound to it even in the moment of recognition, is brought face-to-face with Nothingness.[45] And it is the very grasp of a unique historical opportunity, different from all others, which nevertheless becomes a paradigm of what all human freedom is, in the awe-inspiring moment in which there is acceptance of responsibility for humanity as a whole.[46]

45. Heidegger, "What is Metaphysics?" *op. cit.*, pp. 369 ff.

    If Heidegger's later historicism is accepted—of which, however, "What is Metaphysics" would seem to show no signs—existential anxiety discloses, not a transhistorical limit of human being, but merely an historical limit of an age for which "God is dead" (Cf. Heidegger, *Holzwege*, pp. 193 ff. and especially p. 202).

46. Cf. J. P. Sartre, *Existentialism* (New York: Philosophical Library, 1947), pp. 19 ff.

    Our analysis of the dialectical relation between situation and situated self-making, in its application to the human situation, is enough to

So much for the existential concept of human situation. We must now consider two of its implications, which are of the utmost importance for our present purpose. The first of these is startling indeed. It is the need for a radical revision of the whole doctrine of human self-making.

So long as one grants only the natural situation one admits, to be sure, an other-than-man, as a condition of human self-making. But this other does not constitute, in any way, human being insofar as it is distinctively human. And so long as one grants only, in addition, the historical situation, one does indeed admit something other than self-making which contributes to the constitution of its very humanity; for self-making integrates part of the historical other into its own self, and without this other it could not constitute itself at

refute the widespread view that existential philosophy is fatalistic—a view which implies that human being is the mere product of what situates it. "Existential limitation" and "existential freedom," "standing-out-into-Nothingness" and "being challenged to act authentically" are correlative, not mutually exclusive terms.

all. But the historical other is not, after all, other-than-human but merely other than the particular self-making which it situates. In short, so long as only natural and historical situation are granted, as necessary conditions of human self-making, the conditions admitted do not threaten the autonomy of self-making itself. Human being, *qua* being and *qua* human, can be understood as at least collectively a wholly autonomous human product.

But this is no longer possible once the concept of human situation is accepted. For on the one hand, the humanly situating, like the naturally situating, is not human. On the other hand, it contributes, like the historically situating, to the constitution of man insofar as he is distinctively human. This does not mean that the human situation reduces human being to a mere product; for like every situation, the human situation must stop short of this. But it does mean that the humanly situated must be something less than, and qualitatively different from, an autonomous self-making. For like every situation, the human situation is other than what it situates and yet enters into its internal constitution. But the other in this case is radically other than human being, and yet helps constitute it *qua* human.

This, then, is the radical revision required by the concept of human situation of the doctrine of human self-making: *human being must be understood as something more than a mere product, and yet as something less than a self-making. Instead of a self-constituting, it must rather be the accepting or choosing of something already constituted, and yet also not constituted, because the accepting or choosing is part of its essence.* Thus once more we have come upon a dialectical relation between the situating and the situated. But in the present case—that of the humanly situating and the humanly situated—this dialectic focuses on the relation between the self *qua* accepted and the self *qua* accepting, or between the self that is chosen and the self that does the choosing.

This dialectic is of the greatest subtlety. The self that is chosen must already be a self, for otherwise the self that chooses would not choose but make itself. And yet the chosen self cannot be a self, ready-made apart from the choice, for then there would be no essential choice; and the self as a whole would be a mere product. Correspondingly, the self that chooses must originate in its act of choice, for otherwise it could not choose itself but only this or that. And yet if it wholly originated in its act of self-choice it would be self-production. What emerges from this dialectic is the distinction—fundamental in every form of existential thought—between self and *authentic* self. The self is self whether or not it chooses itself. But only through self-choice does it become authentic self.[47]

47. The following passage deserves to be quoted in full: "But what is it I choose? Is it this thing or that? No, for I choose absolutely, and the absoluteness of my choice is expressed precisely by the fact that I have not chosen this or that. I choose the absolute. But what is the absolute? It is myself in my eternal validity. . . . But what, then, is this self of mine? If I were required to define this, my first answer would be: it is the most abstract of all things, and yet at the same time it is the most concrete—it is freedom. . . .

However the dialectic of self and authentic self may further be developed, it

He chooses himself, not in a finite sense (for then this 'self' would be something finite along with other things finite), but in an absolute sense; and yet, in fact, he chooses himself and not another. This self which he then chooses is infinitely concrete, for it is in fact himself, and yet it is absolutely distinct from his former self, for he has chosen it absolutely. This self did not exist previously, for it came into existence by means of the choice, and yet it did exist, for it was in fact 'himself.' *In this case choice performs at one and the same time two dialectical movements: that which is chosen does not exist and comes into existence with the choice; that which is chosen exists, otherwise there would not be a choice.* For in case what I chose did not exist but absolutely came into existence with the choice, I would not be choosing, I would be creating; but I do not create myself, I choose myself. Therefore, while nature is created out of nothing, while I myself as immediate personality am created out of nothing, as a free spirit I am born out of the principle of contradiction, or born by the fact that I choose myself." Kierkegaard, *Either/ Or, trans. Lowrie,* (Princeton: Princeton University Press, 1944), II, 179 ff. [my italics] Cf. also Jaspers, *Philosophie,* pp. 463 ff.

It must be noted that the "absolute" to which the Kierkegaard passage refers is not Hegel's Absolute; and that whenever he refers to human being as a synthesis of finiteness and infinitude his meaning is different from that of Hegel, whose is clear that the replacement of the doctrine of self-making with a doctrine of self-

terminology he is apt to borrow. Because, unlike Hegel, he regards human being as existentially limited by its human situation, his human "infinitude" consists, not of identification with the Hegelian Absolute, but merely of recognition and free acceptance of its own finitude, which, if authentically performed, is its "absolute."

Confusion with the traditional terms "essence" and "existence" has given rise to the view that "existence," as understood in existential philosophy, is wholly unstructured, "essence" consisting of any structure which an individual may arbitrarily choose to adopt. Sartre's "existence precedes essence" (*op. cit.* p. 18), quoted out of context and used as a slogan, may have furthered this view. But it is wholly mistaken. A wholly unstructured existence would not be a self at all; and a choice of self made on this basis would make the distinction between authentic and unauthentic choice wholly groundless. Yet this distinction is insisted on by every existential thinker, Sartre included. Unless all human existence had *qua* human a common structure, how could Sartre insist, barely two pages after stating that "existence precedes essence," that in an authentic choice an individual must assume responsibility for all men?

Existential "existence," then, differs from traditional "existence" not merely in referring to human existence only. This is generally recognized. It also differs in having a structure of its own. If "existence" is nevertheless distinguished choosing has in turn a most weighty consequence concerning metaphysics as a whole.

from "essence," it is because the structure of existence cannot be an object of cognition apart from acts of choosing, and because these latter acts have a structure of their own. Because they do have such a structure, all attempts to understand the structure of existence must in some way alter that structure. But there is a "true" and a "false" altering. The former authentically faces up to existence instead of being in unauthentic flight from it. That is, the "true" altering must be one which is not an altering—a conclusion which leads back to the dialectic of self-choice.

Kierkegaard's "altering which is not an altering" does not entail the absurdities that our formulation may seem to suggest. It does not deny, for example, that my historical opportunities remain unrealized unless I myself realize them; that free historical acting is an "altering which *is* an altering." But if I am humanly as well as historically situated, such free acting, radically considered, is part of an altering which is *not* an altering. For the historical opportunities which I realize were mine before my realization of them; and only if I choose them *as* mine is my realization of them part of an authentic act of self-choice, rather than, to use Kierkegaard's language, a mere choice of this or that.

For much of the foregoing, cf. Heidegger, "Ueber den Humanismus," in *Platons Lehre von der Wahrheit* (Bern: Verlag A. Francke Ag., 1947), pp. 70 ff., especially p. 71: "Das deutet

So long as human being is understood as a self-making, metaphysics as a human enter-

an, dass sich jetzt das 'Wesen' weder aus dem esse essentiae, noch aus dem esse existentiae, sondern aus dem Ek-statischen des Daseins bestimmt. *Als der Ek-sistierende steht der Mensch das Da-sein aus, indem er das Da als die Lichtung des Seins in die 'Sorge' nimmt. Das Da-sein selbst aber ist das 'geworfene.' Es west im Wurf des Seins als des schickend Geschicklichen."* [my italics]

Because of the misunderstanding that existential "existence" is structureless, existential ethics is often regarded as nihilistic. But existential ethics never denies objective right and wrong; it merely insists that these can be discovered only in the existential situation, and hence that their discovery is shot through with risk. Franz Kafka tells the story of an individual who, though desiring to find his road to the moral law, yet fails to do so until the end of his life, both because he cannot know the right road before embarking on it, and because there is no one else to join him. It is only at the end of his life—when there is no longer time for choosing either right or wrong—that he discovers that no one else could have joined him on his road because the road was for him alone. (*Vor Dem Gesetz* [Berlin: Schocken Verlag, 1934], pp. 8 ff.). What gives poignancy to Kafka's story is precisely these two factors, taken in conjunction: that there is only one right road for a man, and that he cannot know whether it is right except by embarking on it.

prise must clearly be regarded as part of the self-making process. And this in turn compels one at least to entertain the possibility that the truths known by metaphysics too are affected by human self-making, that man has at least a share in creating the realm to the knowledge of which his metaphysics rises.[48]

But once human being is understood as a humanly situated self-choosing, this possibility is at once wholly excluded. For what situates man humanly is not produced by man but on the contrary the condition of all human producing. And in rising to metaphysics man recognizes this fact; but in recognizing it he recognizes the otherness of the Other that situates him. This Other is the Other *par excellence.*

In this recognition the Other must, and yet cannot, remain wholly unknown. It must remain unknown, for if human being were to know It it would cease to be situ-

48. This possibility is fully explored by Hegel, for whom philosophy is both the realization and part of the self-realization of the Absolute.

ated by It. Hence all supposed knowledge of this Other is but pseudo-knowledge, due to pseudo-detachment from, or pseudo-transcendence of, the human situation. And yet this Other cannot remain wholly unknown. For to know its otherness is to have passed beyond simple ignorance. We have seen that existential metaphysics originates in the recognition of man's human situation, as a dialectical mystery. We now see that this metaphysics culminates in pointing, as to a vastly greater mystery, to the ultimate Other which situates man humanly. And this pointing-to is itself dialectical. It expresses an ignorance which knows the grounds of this ignorance, or a knowledge which knows that it is ignorant, and why. The Other that is pointed to thus remains undefined, and is yet given names. But the names express Mystery. They do not disclose It.[49]

49.   It must be borne in mind, however, that pointing-to-the-Other, the last achievement of unaided philosophical thought, need not be regarded in existential thought as necessarily the last achievement of man: if the Other is God who reveals Himself. On this point, cf., e.g., Schelling's dis-

CONCLUSION

In this lecture, we have endeavoured to show that the doctrine of historicity requires the assumption that human being is a self-constituting process; and what doctrinal provisions must be made once that initial assumption is granted. But why should that initial assumption be made at all? Why should human being be regarded as a self-constituting process? This is a question which we have thus far failed to raise. Hence our whole discourse, thus far, is a mere fragment; as it were, an incomplete metaphysical hypothesis.

It must, we fear, remain such an hypothesis. For it is much too late to deal properly with a question which requires solid treatment in its own right. And our concluding remarks can do no more than stress the need for such a treatment.

The doctrine of human being as a self-making was first put forward, under the

tinction between "negative" and "positive" philosophy (cf. my article referred to in note 24), and Buber, *Eclipse of God* (New York: Harper Torchbook, 1952), p. 50.

influence of Kant, in opposition to three
competing doctrines; and against two of
these it won a resounding victory. The
first was the kind of substantialism which,
regarding the human self as no less ready-
made than matter, offered a mere carica-
ture of selfhood. The second was the
Humean kind of mental process which,
being a simple rather than a self-constituting process, does not deserve to be called
mental at all. To be sure, the war on these
two doctrines has had to be refought again
and again. For empiricism has the habit
of raising its head, no matter how often
and how decisively it is refuted; and the
same is true of attempts to reduce the self
to the non-self which, however disguised
as naturalism, evolutionism or behavior-
ism, are never very far from crude mate-
rialism. The war has always had to be refought; but it has always been rewon: by
Heidegger, Jaspers and Collingwood in our
own age no less decisively than by Fichte,
Schelling and Hegel in theirs.[50]

50. Kant's case against Hume is too well known

But the doctrine of human self-making
was originally asserted also against a third

to require documentation. (For a clear statement
of Kantian "self-identity," cf. H. J. Paton, "Self-
identity," in *In Defence of Reason* (London:
Hutchinson, 1951], pp. 99 ff., especially p. 102.)
For the case against the reduction of "being-for-
itself" to "being-in-itself," cf. Fichte, *Werke*, I,
435 ff., English trans., *Journal of Speculative
Philosophy*, I, (1867), 29 ff.

Kant, though inspiring the doctrine of human
self-making in his successors, did not himself
accept it. "Even as to himself, a man cannot pre-
tend to know what he is in himself from the
knowledge he has by internal sensation. For *as
he does not as it were create himself*, and does
not come by the conception of himself apriori
but empirically, it naturally follows that he can
obtain his knowledge even of himself only by
inner sense, and consequently only through the
appearance of his nature and the way in which
his consciousness is affected." *Werke*, IV, 451,
trans. Abbott, *Kant's Theory of Ethics*, (London:
Longmans, Green and Company, 1889), 70 ff.
[my italics].

Then why did Fichte accept the doctrine of
human self-making, the first post-Kantian philo-
sopher to do so? Three reasons may be cited for
Kant's refusal to accept it, and of these the third
is decisive. First, he regards natural inclinations
as *ultimately* given, and hence as morally innocent. Secondly, he regards moral law too as ultimately given, and merely appropriated in human acts of self-legislation. (This interpretation

doctrine: the classical doctrine of a permanent human nature. And the history of this

is controversial, but we cannot here pause to defend it.) Thirdly, he regards the metaphysical knowledge of man as a task which transcends human power. If he is left with two human "natures"—the empirical and the intelligible—despite the fact that there can ultimately be only one man viewed from two perspectives (e.g., Abbott, *op. cit.*, 69 ff.), it is because of the impossibility of rising to an absolute standpoint in which the two perspectives are synthesized.

Fichte disagrees with Kant on all three points, although he is not fully aware of the fact of disagreement. First, natural inclinations are not ultimately given; for they are not innocent, and they are destined to moral transformation and eventual elimination. (Cf. *supra* note 32). Secondly, moral law is produced by the self-legislating self who, in moral action, has a share in the creation of the intelligible world. Thirdly, metaphysical cognition of the self by the self is not impossible, although it is knowledge of a kind quite different from that asserted in pre-Kantian metaphysics. In intellectual intuition "I know something because I do it." Without this creative intuition there would be no awareness of self-identity, and without the awareness, no self-identity; but without self-identity the self would not be a self at all. (*Werke*, I, 460 ff., *Journal of Speculative Philosophy*, I, 83 ff., 139).

It must be added, however, that for Fichte it is one thing to assert the indispensability of an intellectual intuition which at once knows and creates, quite another to explain the conditions of conflict, unlike the other two, has been complex and ambiguous.

Kant's immediate followers did not object primarily, or even at all, to the notion of human permanence. What they did object to was the notion of a human nature, that is, to the notion of a reality ready-made prior to the self's own acting, and yet fully human. Thus Fichte held that the self had to be wholly self-produced in order to be a self at all; and that to regard it as in any sense constituted by another—even if that Other were God—was both metaphysically and morally intolerable.[51]

its possibility. (*Werke*, I, 465, *Journal of Speculative Philosophy*, I, 86.) Fichte accepts idealism as the only theory capable of explaining that possibility. But subsequent developments, down to existentialism, show that the doctrine of human self-making is not necessarily bound up with idealism.

51. Cf., e.g., Fichte's "Ueber den Grund unseres Glaubens an eine goettliche Weltregierung" (*Werke*, V, 177 ff.), an essay which became famous because it unleashed the famous "atheism controversy." While defending belief in Providence, Fichte assails the doctrine of a created self: "Nothing other than the self may be assumed as the ground in terms of which it is to

But subsequent history shows a steady
retreat from the extreme Fichtean position.
Already Schelling and Hegel insist that the
self requires a background other than itself
for its self-constitution, although they are
idealistic enough to believe that in the
highest form of the self's self-constitution
no aspect of otherness remains.[52] A far
more radical retreat is carried out by Kierkegaard. Kierkegaard lays no less stress
than his predecessors on the self as a process of self-activity. Possibly he even exceeds them in emphasis. For that being-a-
self is a responsibility rather than a given
fact is a thesis which is stated in his writings with unmatched pathos. At the same

be explained. . . . For how can the self explain
itself—nay, even just wish to explain itself—without thereby going beyond itself and thus ceasing
to be a self? Wherever we even just ask for an
explanation there can no longer be a pure (absolutely free and self-dependent) self; for all
explanation makes dependent." (p. 180).

52.   These forms are art, religion and philosophy.
In these manifestations of spiritual life the self
transcends selfhood itself. This implies that, so
long as the self remains a self at all, it remains
dependent on a natural background which is
other-than-self.

time, he radically breaks with the idealism of his predecessors. And the essence of the break lies in his insistence on existential limitations which, being universally human, define man's very humanity. Hence idealistic self-making reduces itself to existential self-choosing: to the appropriating acceptance of a gift which is, and yet is not, fully real before the gift is accepted.

Viewing the history of this retreat, one may well wonder whether the whole doctrine of human self-making must not be abandoned altogether, in favor of the classical doctrine of a human nature. After all, even Aristotle did not deny that a specifically human characteristic such as rationality is not actual until man himself actualizes it; yet this did not prevent him from regarding it as a potentiality grounded in human nature. What if speculative thought can contemplate the human situation, as described by existential philosophers, and identify a human nature as its ontological ground?

But at least one crucial objection would be made to such a project by thinkers such as Kierkegaard, Jaspers, and Buber. They would object that the self cannot *qua* self become an object of speculative thought; and that to treat it as such is incompatible with the demands to be made in behalf of selfhood. They would insist that the human situation can only be existentially encountered, not made an object of detached thought, and that hence any attempt to discover a human nature as the ground of the human situation is doomed from the start. And when offered a concept of human nature, no matter what particular concept it might be, they would no doubt dismiss it, as a mere objectifying construction.

Does the classical doctrine of a human nature have the resources to meet this objection? More generally, can it assimilate the insights into selfhood, achieved from Kant and Fichte down to Heidegger and Collingwood, without suffering collapse in this process of assimilation? Can it, perhaps, mount a counterattack, based on the indispensability of speculative thought? For that existential philosophy cannot wholly dispense with such thought is all too obvious.[53] These are vital questions; and they invite what might well become the most profound metaphysical dialogue in our time.

One fact, above all, augurs well for such a dialogue. In its existential form, the doctrine of human self-making has been driven to the conclusion that a reality other than man has a share in the constitution of human being *qua* being and *qua* human: a reality which cannot be either nature which is less than human, or historical action which is only human. But this is a view which the classical doctrine of human nature has held or implied all along.

53. It need hardly be said that this whole lecture has moved in the realm of speculative discourse; and that, unless it is to cease to be philosophy, all existential philosophy must in part move in that realm. But this gives rise to two questions: can existential philosophy justify its own movement in this realm; and precisely how must speculative discourse be related to what is *not* speculative discourse but immediate existential commitment — "foundering," "encounter with Nothingness," "existential decision" and the like? It is no exaggeration to say that the future of existential philosophy *as philosophy* depends on its ability to answer these questions.

Epilogue

The British Museum Library possesses a Schelling volume with marginal notes by no less a person than Samuel Taylor Coleridge. On page nine of the volume Schelling writes: "Ich bin, weil ich bin. Das ergreift jeden ploetzlich." "I am because I am. This truth seizes hold, all of a sudden, of everyone." Writing under Fichte's influence, Schelling here asserts that the self is the absolute source of its self-constitution, and that in great moments it becomes intuitively aware of this fact. Coleridge comments, naively and yet with the utmost profundity: "Jeden?" "Everyone? I doubt it. Many may say: I am because God made me."[54]

54. *Schriften* (Landshut: Bei Philipp Krüell, 1809), p. 9, *Werke*, I, 168.

The Aquinas Lectures

Published by the Marquette University Press,
Milwaukee 3, Wisconsin

St. Thomas and the Life of Learning (1937) by
the late Fr. John F. McCormick, S.J., professor of philosophy, Loyola University.

St. Thomas and the Gentiles (1938) by Mortimer J. Adler, Ph.D., director of the Institute
of Philosophical Research, San Francisco,
Calif.

St. Thomas and the Greeks (1939) by Anton C.
Pegis, Ph.D., former president and present
professor of the Pontifical Institute of Mediaeval Studies, Toronto.

The Nature and Functions of Authority (1940)
by Yves Simon, Ph.D., professor of philosophy of social thought, University of Chicago.

St. Thomas and Analogy (1941) by Fr. Gerald
B. Phelan, Ph.D., professor of philosophy, St.
Michael's College, Toronto.

St. Thomas and the Problem of Evil (1942) by
Jacques Maritain, Ph.D., professor *emeritus*
of philosophy, Princeton University.

Humanism and Theology (1943) by Werner Jaeger, Ph.D., Litt.D., University professor, Harvard University.

The Nature and Origins of Scientism (1944) by John Wellmuth.

Cicero in the Courtroom of St. Thomas Aquinas (1945) by the late E. K. Rand, Ph.D., Litt.D., LL.D., Pope professor of Latin, *emeritus,* Harvard University.

St. Thomas and Epistemology (1946) by Fr. Louis-Marie Regis, O.P., Th.L., Ph.D., director of the Albert the Great Institute of Mediaeval Studies, University of Montreal.

St. Thomas and the Greek Moralists (1947, Spring) by Vernon J. Bourke, Ph.D., professor of philosophy, St. Louis University, St. Louis, Missouri.

History of Philosophy and Philosophical Education (1947, Fall) by Étienne Gilson of the *Académie française,* director of studies and professor of the history of Mediaeval philosophy, Pontifical Institute of Mediaeval Studies, Toronto.

The Natural Desire for God (1948) by Fr. William R. O'Connor, S.T.L., Ph.D., former professor of dogmatic theology, St. Joseph's Seminary, Dunwoodie, N.Y.

St. Thomas and the World State (1949) by Robert M. Hutchins, former Chancellor of the University of Chicago.

Method in Metaphysics (1950) by Fr. Robert J. Henle, S.J., dean of the graduate school, St. Louis University, St. Louis, Missouri.

Wisdom and Love in St. Thomas Aquinas (1951) by Etienne Gilson of the *Académie française,* director of studies and professor of the history of Mediaeval philosophy, Pontifical Institute of Mediaeval Studies, Toronto.

The Good in Existential Metaphysics (1952) by Elizabeth G. Salmon, associate professor of philosophy in the graduate school, Fordham University.

St. Thomas and the Object of Geometry (1953) by Vincent Edward Smith, Ph.D., professor of philosophy, University of Notre Dame.

Realism and Nominalism Revisited (1954) by Henry Veatch, Ph.D., professor of philosophy, Indiana University.

Imprudence in St. Thomas Aquinas (1955) by Charles J. O'Neil, Ph.D., professor of philosophy, Marquette University.

The Truth That Frees (1956) by Fr. Gerard Smith, S.J., Ph.D., professor and chairman of the department of philosophy, Marquette University.

St. Thomas and the Future of Metaphysics (1957) by Fr. Joseph Owens, C.Ss.R., associate professor of philosophy, Pontifical Institute of Mediaeval Studies, Toronto.

Thomas and the Physics of 1958: A Confrontation (1958) by Henry Margenau, Ph.D., Eugene Higgins professor of physics and natural philosophy, Yale University.

Metaphysics and Ideology (1959) by Wm. Oliver Martin, professor of philosophy, University of Rhode Island.

Language, Truth and Poetry (1960) by Victor M. Hamm, Ph.D., professor of English, Marquette University.

Metaphysics and Historicity (1961) by Emil L. Fackenheim, Ph.D., associate professor of philosophy, University of Toronto.

Uniform format, cover and binding.